Human Resource Management and Army Recruiting

Analyses of Policy Options

James N. Dertouzos, Steven Garber

Prepared for the United States Army
Approved for public release; distribution unlimited

RAND ARROYO CENTER

The research in this report was sponsored by the United States Army under Contract No. DASW01-01-C-0003.

Library of Congress Cataloging-in-Publication Data

Dertouzos, James N., 1950–
    Human resource management and Army recruiting : analyses of policy options / James N. Dertouzos, Steven Garber.
      p. cm.
    "MG-433."
    Includes bibliographical references.
    ISBN-13: 978-0-8330-4004-6 (pbk. : alk. paper)
    1. United States. Army—Recruiting, enlistment, etc. 2. United States. Army—Personnel management. I. Garber, Steven, 1950– II. Title.

    UB323.D438 2006
    355.2'23620973—dc22

                                                            2006027016

The RAND Corporation is a nonprofit research organization providing objective analysis and effective solutions that address the challenges facing the public and private sectors around the world. RAND's publications do not necessarily reflect the opinions of its research clients and sponsors.

RAND® is a registered trademark.

Published 2006 by the RAND Corporation
1776 Main Street, P.O. Box 2138, Santa Monica, CA 90407-2138
1200 South Hayes Street, Arlington, VA 22202-5050
4570 Fifth Avenue, Suite 600, Pittsburgh, PA 15213-2665
RAND URL: http://www.rand.org/
To order RAND documents or to obtain additional information, contact
Distribution Services: Telephone: (310) 451-7002;
Fax: (310) 451-6915; Email: order@rand.org

Preface

This report documents research methods, findings, and policy conclusions from a project analyzing human resource management options for improving recruiting production. This work will interest those involved in the day-to-day management of recruiting resources as well as researchers and analysts engaged in analyses of military enlistment behavior. This research was sponsored by the Assistant Secretary of the Army (Manpower and Reserve Affairs) and was conducted in RAND Arroyo Center's Manpower and Training Program. RAND Arroyo Center, part of the RAND Corporation, is a federally funded research and development center sponsored by the United States Army.

The Project Unique Identification Code (PUIC) for the project that produced this document is SAMRH02005.

For more information on RAND Arroyo Center, contact the Director of Operations (telephone 310-393-0411, extension 6419; FAX 310-451-6952; email Marcy_Agmon@rand.org), or visit Arroyo's web site at http://www.rand.org/ard/.

Contents

Figures

Tables

Summary

The U.S. Army Recruiting Command (USAREC) is charged with providing the Army with an ongoing flow of qualified volunteers adequate to meet future active-duty accession requirements. Success is highly dependent on several factors that USAREC can control and several others that it cannot control. Among the latter are manpower requirements (demand for accessions) as well as supply factors such as market demographics, alternative labor market and educational opportunities for youth, and attitudes about military service.

Whatever the prevailing supply and demand conditions, however, policymakers have several policy levers for increasing the flow of enlistment contracts. Most manpower research has focused on the roles of recruiting resources such as military pay, enlistment benefits, advertising programs, and numbers of recruiters. Although such policy instruments have demonstrable expansion effects, they are quite costly to use. For example, Dertouzos and Garber (2003) provide marginal cost estimates of increasing high-quality enlistments via expansions in military pay, the recruiting force, and advertising ranging between $13,000 and $60,000 per additional high-quality recruit.

In contrast, there is little available research on a range of human resource management policies that are capable of enhancing the productivity of the recruiting force. These policies include personnel selection and training, recruiter assignment, performance measurement, and the design of incentive systems that motivate recruiters to be more productive. More effective policies in these domains could increase enlistments for little, if any, additional cost.

This report details research designed to develop new insights to help guide future recruiter-management policies. The research involves econometric analyses of three large and rich datasets.

Methods

In Chapter Two, we analyze determinants of the productivity of individual regular Army recruiters in enlisting both high- and lower-quality youth from 1998 to 2000. During this period, recruiters were missioned and rewarded on an individual basis. The data include monthly observations for more than 10,000 recruiters and a total of more than 130,000 observations on recruiter-month pairs. This analysis probes the characteristics of recruiters that are associated with higher and lower rates of productivity and how productivity relates to matches between recruiter characteristics and the characteristics of the markets (station areas) to which they are assigned. The analyses provide insights relevant to selection of soldiers for assignment to recruiting duty as well as the types of markets to which recruiters with specific characteristics might be best assigned.

In Chapter Three, we analyze data for the 30-month period from January 2001 through June 2003. During this period, all stations were missioned at the station level and recruiting success was defined in terms of meeting missions as a team. Thus, the unit of analysis is a station-month, and the dataset includes information for roughly 1,600 stations and a total of more than 42,000 station-month pairs. This analysis focuses on factors determining the probability that a station will meet all of its regular Army missions, plus any losses from the Delayed Entry Program (DEP) charged during the month, in which case recruiters who wrote at least one contract could be eligible for station-level bonus points. (Almost 60 percent of stations also have U.S. Army Reserve (USAR) missions; these stations must meet both their regular Army and USAR missions for recruiters to be eligible for station-level bonus points.) This analysis also probes the extent to which allocations of regular Army missions to stations achieves equity across recruiters in the sense of equalizing the probabilities of meeting these missions.

Chapters Four and Five analyze the same data used in Chapter Three, applying models developed to focus on missioning policies to promote productivity (efficiency) in regular Army recruiting. In particular, we estimate models determining the number of high-quality enlistments by stations on a monthly basis and use the results to simulate or predict the effects of alternative missioning policies during the period covered by the data. The models separately identify the determinants of recruiter effort and the determinants of the quality of a station's market area. The key ideas underlying the model are that (a) contract production depends on the quality of the station's market area and the effort level of the recruiters, (b) effort is likely to increase as missions become more difficult, as long as they aren't so difficult that they discourage recruiters and undermine motivation, and (c) in better markets, less effort is required for recruiters to sign high-quality youth.

In Chapter Six, we study various relationships between recruiting and the career paths of soldiers. More specifically, we use a dataset on nearly 90,000 enlisted personnel who entered the Army during the ten-year period comprising fiscal years 1987 through 1996 to analyze several outcomes, including which soldiers became recruiters, how long recruiters stayed in recruiting, and how recruiting duty and productivity in recruiting affected promotion to the grades of E-6 and E-7 and the likelihood of remaining in the Army until 2003.

Key Findings

The analysis in Chapter Two relates numbers of high-quality and total enlistments to market characteristics, traditional supply factors, and attributes of recruiters. The findings for the period 1998 to 2000, when missions and award points were assigned on an individual basis, include the following.

- On average, an increased mission of one high- or low-quality contract resulted in an increase of only 0.12 contracts. In contrast, estimates reported in Chapter Four imply three times as much responsiveness during 2001 to 2003, a period when missions were assigned to stations, missions per recruiter were lower, and the general recruiting environment may have been better. This suggests that teamwork was effective during the latter period, that responsiveness to mission is higher when the difficulty of making mission is lower, or both.
- Our estimates enable us to rank groups of factors in terms of their importance in explaining variations in enlistment outcomes. Missions and market and demographic factors are most important in this regard. In decreasing order of importance, other important factors are nationwide differences in the recruiting environment over time, measured personal attributes of recruiters, station size, and region of the country.
- Regarding relationships between specific recruiter attributes and productivity, some of which can be helpful in selecting soldiers for assignment to USAREC, there are several noteworthy patterns. First, younger male recruiters with dependents tend to be especially productive. Second, recruiters whose pre-recruiting military occupational specialties (MOSs) are in technical, combat, or intelligence areas tend to be more productive than those whose pre-recruiting MOS is in logistics. Third, recruiter Armed Forces Qualification Test (AFQT) scores and levels of education seem to have no effect on recruiting productivity.
- We also find evidence that unmeasured personal attributes of recruiters account for more of the variation in production levels than do the attributes that we were able to measure. Potentially important unmeasured attributes are soldiers' talent for selling, their general levels of motivation and energy, and their time-management skills.
- We also find strong patterns regarding relationships between recruiter attributes and the characteristics of market areas of the stations to which they are assigned. Broadly stated, recruiters are more productive when their characteristics are similar to those of

many of the youth in their market areas. For example, recruiters assigned to stations in their home states are more productive. Moreover, African American recruiters are more productive than other recruiters in areas where African Americans comprise large proportions of the local population. Female recruiters are more effective in signing women, although they appear to be less effective in signing men.

- Recruiters in stations with more than one regular Army recruiter tend to be less productive than those in one-recruiter stations, and these differences are substantial. For example, stations with six or more "on-production, regular Army" (OPRA) recruiters are on average 14 and 17 percent less productive than one-recruiter stations in enlisting high-quality candidates and all candidates, respectively. Productivity differences associated with station sizes might reflect unmeasured factors such as attributes of soldiers assigned to one-recruiter stations and greater familiarity between recruiters and members of smaller communities, including high school counselors, coaches, and other youth influencers. These differences may also reflect differences in unmeasured aspects of attitudes toward the military between larger and smaller communities.

The analysis in Chapter Three uses data from 2001 to 2003, a period when missions were assigned on a station-level basis and award points were available for success as a team, including both regular Army and USAR recruiters, if any. The focus is on how station-level factors affected the probability that a station met all three of its regular Army production goals (i.e., grad alphas, senior alphas, and others[1]) taking account of substitution rules and DEP losses. Key findings include the following.

- Our estimates regarding the roles of traditional supply factors are broadly consistent with earlier results.

---

[1] "Alpha" denotes a high-aptitude recruit—an enlistee who scored in categories I through IIIA on the AFQT. "Grad" and "senior" refer to high school graduates and high school seniors, respectively.

- Stations met their regular Army goals during one-third of the station-months in our sample. If their missions for grad alphas had been one contract higher, the probability of meeting these missions would have fallen to about 17 percent; the analogous figure for adding a senior alpha mission is 20 percent. Thus, the data indicate that recruiters have a more difficult time locating and signing additional grad alphas than senior alphas.
- Adding one contract to the mission for "others" (than grad or senior alphas) lowers the probability of success from the baseline 33 percent to 28 percent. Comparing this result to those just reported for additional high-quality missions suggests that high-quality contracts are about three times as difficult to obtain as lower-quality ones. Since the ratio of award points for high-quality contracts to lower-quality contracts is only two to one, this suggests that recruiters are not being given adequate incentives to sign high-quality youth, considering the relative costs of producing the two types of contracts.

Equity in missioning is important in and of itself and because if recruiters perceive unfairness, it could undermine morale and effort and thereby reduce productivity. Accordingly, much of the analysis reported in Chapter Three focuses on the extent to which missions give stations equal chances of success in meeting their regular Army goals. Our analysis provides insights about types of factors and specific factors within each type that are associated with differences across stations in the probability of succeeding in this sense. Our key findings related to equity of missioning include the following.

- Stations with USAR missions meet their regular Army goals almost as often as stations without USAR missions (34.6 percent versus 37.2 percent). But stations with USAR missions succeed according to the Army's definition of team success—i.e., meeting all regular Army and USAR missions—much less frequently than do stations without USAR missions, which in their cases requires meeting only regular Army missions. In particular, stations with USAR missions succeed only 16.7 percent of the time as compared with 37.2 percent for stations that don't have USAR missions.

- The most important set of factors accounting for differences in the probability of success relative to regular Army goals is the demographics of the stations' market areas. The following three sets of factors are each roughly 75 percent as important as demographics: (a) factors that differ over time but are largely the same nationwide within months, such as youth attitudes, (b) numbers of USAR recruiters and the levels of USAR missions, and (c) supply or market variables (qualified military available (QMA)[2] per OPRA, the level and change in the local unemployment rate, and the level of civilian wages in the local area).

- The analysis also details characteristics of markets associated with higher and lower probabilities of success in meeting regular Army missions. These findings provide guidance about how missions could be adjusted to promote equity across stations. To promote equity, missions should be decreased in relative terms for stations with: (a) relatively high proportions of veterans aged 43 to 54 and 65 to 72 in the state population; (b) large proportions of Hispanics, African Americans, and children living in poverty in the local population; and (c) relatively high USAR missions per OPRA recruiter, holding the number of USAR recruiters constant. Moreover, to equalize probabilities of success over seasons, missions should be lowered in March and May.

- To promote equity, missions should be increased in relative terms for stations (a) with relatively high proportions of veterans aged 33 to 42 and 56 to 65 in the state population, (b) with more USAR recruiters per OPRA recruiter, holding the USAR missions per OPRA constant, (c) in the South and, to a lesser extent, in the North Central region, and (d) with higher unemployment rates. Moreover, to equalize probabilities of success over seasons, missions should be increased in December.

---

[2] QMA counts net out from youth population totals the estimated numbers of youth in college and those who are ineligible for military service for physical reasons or because of criminal records.

We also analyzed the extent to which succeeding relative to regular Army missions reflects random factors that recruiters cannot control, an issue that is crucial for assessing station performance. For example, one might be inclined to observe the number of consecutive months a station fails to meet its regular Army mission and intervene after a particular number of months. Our analysis reveals potential pitfalls in such a procedure. More specifically, we compare the proportion of stations that would be expected to fail due to chance, given their stations' missions and the quality of their markets, for a specific number of consecutive months with the proportions that actually failed. For example, among stations that have failed six months in a row, half would be expected to fail because of pure chance. The analogous proportions for stations failing 3 and 12 months in a row are 82 and 23 percent.

The analyses reported in Chapters Four and Five develop and implement new models and methods designed to decompose production of high-quality contracts into its two major underlying determinants, namely, the quality of the station's market area and the effort levels expended by the station's recruiters to sign high-quality youth. We use the results to simulate the effects of various missioning policies. The key findings are as follows.

- As expected, recruiter effort levels increase at a decreasing rate as the difficulty of meeting the regular Army high-quality goal increases from low levels of difficulty. The evidence is overwhelming, however, that during the sample period, missions were virtually never difficult enough to discourage recruiters to the extent that effort was reduced.
- A station's recent high-quality production relative to high-quality mission is an important determinant of effort levels and the responsiveness of effort to increases in missions. More specifically, stations with higher ratios of high-quality enlistments to high-quality missions over a 12-month period ending three months before the current month expended considerably more effort, and their effort levels were considerably more responsive to increases in missions. We believe that these findings are attributable to

higher morale, confidence, or both among recruiters in stations that have recently been more successful.

- These results suggest that during January 2001 through June 2003 there were unexploited opportunities to increase high-quality enlistments in two general ways: (a) reallocating the aggregate high-quality missions differently over stations and over months, and (b) increasing aggregate high-quality missions.

- Regarding reallocating the actual national-level mission over stations and months, policy simulations suggest that the potential improvements were significant but not dramatic. In particular, a reallocation of only 2 percent of total missions could have increased total high-quality enlistments by 1.0 percent. An optimal reallocation (involving about a third of all missions) could have resulted in a 2.7 percent productivity increase.

- Regarding increases in the aggregate high-quality mission, our simulations suggest quite substantial potential gains. For example, during the time period studied, increasing the monthly high-quality mission by one contract for the half of stations that would be most responsive—which involves a 15.5 percent increase in aggregate high-quality missions—is predicted to have had the potential to increase high-quality enlistments by 7.4 percent. Whether such gains would be possible in the current recruiting environment is unknown.

- Our microeconomic theory underlying the econometric models implies that there is a conflict between equity—in the form of equalizing the difficulty of making mission—and efficiency—in the form of maximizing expected contracts—if and only if effort functions differ across stations. The strong evidence that effort functions do differ (according to the degree of recent success) indicates that there is such a conflict.

- Market quality varies considerably, and in intuitively sensible ways, with variations in dozens of variables representing local economic conditions, market demographics, seasonal effects, the size and age distribution of the veteran population, and the region of the country.

- Due to differences across stations and over time in market quality and other factors, the additional effort required to sign another high-quality youth varies considerably over stations and months. For example, this effort level is considerably more than twice as high on average for the 20 percent of stations confronting the least favorable conditions than for the 20 percent of stations facing the most favorable conditions. In addition, most of the unexplained variation in productivity of effort across stations is attributable to (a) randomness that averages out within a year, and (b) unmeasured, and perhaps unmeasurable, factors that are specific to individual stations.
- The major factors affecting market quality are as follows, in decreasing order of importance. It takes less effort to sign high-quality youth: (a) in low civilian-wage areas; (b) where QMA per OPRA is high; (c) in markets with the following demographic characteristics—urban, relatively high proportions of non-Catholic Christians, and relatively low proportions of African Americans and children living in poverty; (d) in the months of June, July, September, and October, especially as compared with May; (e) in areas with relatively high proportions of veterans aged less than 43 and relatively low proportions of veterans aged 56 to 65; and (f) in regions other than the Mountain region.
- We also simulated a policy that, in contrast to current policies, doesn't add DEP losses to missions in assessing monthly success. This policy scenario also increases missions equally for all stations to hold total goals constant. The results suggest that about 0.2 percent of production would be lost from such a policy change. This is because DEP losses tend to be higher for stations that have been more productive recently (i.e., signed more contracts in the recent past, and therefore tend to have more enlistees in the DEP), and asking for more from relatively successful stations is effective because such stations are more responsive to increases in missions.
- Missioning all recruiters at the same level for all stations and months would have gained 1 percent in terms of high-quality enlistments relative to the missions that were actually used.

Most of these gains are due to smoothing missions over months, which cannot be done unless aggregate contract requirements are smoothed over months.

Our analysis in Chapter Six of Army careers and recruiting examined several outcomes. The key findings are as follows.

- The roughly 8 percent of soldiers who became recruiters were relatively high quality in terms of indicators such as AFQT scores, high school graduation, and speeds of promotion (before becoming recruiters) to E-4 and E-5. Such factors can increase or decrease the probability of becoming a recruiter by four percentage points, which is very substantial compared with the average of 8 percent.
- Soldiers who had been recruiters were more likely to have been promoted to E-6 and E-7 by 2003, holding other factors constant. See Table S.1.
- Recruiters who were relatively slow in being promoted to E-4 and E-5 were more likely to leave recruiting in less than one year, and those who were promoted relatively quickly to E-4 and E-5 were more likely to stay in recruiting for more than three years.
- We also analyzed the effects of recruiting performance, measured in various ways, on the likelihood of promotion to E-6 and E-7 by 2003. When recruiting performance is defined in terms of tenure, we find that (a) recruiting for less than one year had no effect on subsequent career progression (i.e., there seems to be no penalty for starting recruiting and failing); (b) those who were in recruiting for less than two years, but more than one, had a substantially higher average probability of promotion to E-6 than

Table S.1
Predicted Probabilities of Promotion by 2003,
Recruiters Versus Nonrecruiters: 1991 Entering Cohort

	Probability of Promotion to E-6	Probability of Promotion to E-7
Recruiters	0.892	0.123
Nonrecruiters	0.806	0.099

soldiers who had never recruited (0.88 versus 0.72 for nonrecruiters) and a slightly higher probability of promotion to E-7 (0.055 versus 0.046); (c) recruiting for two to three years relative to one to two years had no effect on promotion prospects; (d) those who recruited for three or more years were substantially more likely to make E-6 and E-7 than soldiers who never recruited, with a 0.94 chance of E-6 (versus 0.72 for nonrecruiters) and 0.176 chance of making E-7 (versus 0.046 for nonrecruiters).

- We find little, if any, effect of contract production levels on promotion rates. However, we find substantial effects of high-quality production ratios (high-quality contracts divided by high-quality missions) at the station and recruiter levels that are above average relative to other stations and recruiters, respectively, during the same time period. For example, recruiters in stations with particularly low relative performance have a 78 percent chance of making E-6, compared with probabilities of 83 percent and 87 percent for recruiters from stations with average and particularly good relative performance, respectively. The corresponding probabilities for promotion to E-7 are 4, 6, and 9 percent.
- We also found that recruiters were substantially more likely to remain in the Army until 2003 than nonrecruiters, with probabilities of 89 and 82 percent, respectively.

Implications for Effective Recruiter Management

Our research demonstrates that various types of human resource management policies can be very helpful in meeting the Army's ambitious recruiting requirements. Although the gains from any individual policy change appear to be modest, implementing several policy changes in combination could save the Army hundreds of millions of dollars annually. Indeed, based on an incremental cost of $6,000 per recruit attracted by increasing recruiters, each one percent increase in high-quality enlistments generated by a more effective management approach could save the Army $3.6 million annually.

In Chapter Seven, we consider implications of our findings for human resource policies in the areas of selecting soldiers for recruiting duty, assigning recruiters to stations, missioning to promote equity across recruiters, missioning to increase recruiting production, using promotions to motivate and reward recruiters, and screening out recruiters who are underproducing.

Our analyses have focused on potential means of improving recruiting outcomes. To consider potential policy changes, however, we adopt the perspective of the U.S. Army, rather than USAREC alone, because many policies that we have found to offer increases in recruiting production may impose costs on other commands. For example, assigning unusually good soldiers to recruiting involves a relatively high burden on the commands losing some of their most highly valued personnel.

Recruiter Selection

- **Some recruiter attributes are very helpful in predicting recruiter productivity.**

Our findings suggest that efforts to identify and measure additional recruiter attributes that are expected to be strong predictors of recruiting success should continue to receive high priority and that data should be developed to enable future empirical verification that these attributes really do have substantial effects on productivity in the field.

- **Young recruiters are more productive.**

By adding about 500 young (under age 30) recruiters and reducing the number of older recruiters (over 35) by the same number, the Army could increase overall productivity by about 1 percent. To decide whether this is a sound policy change, the Army should consider the relative opportunity costs of reassigning younger and more senior personnel, and effects (that are likely to differ by MOS) on younger soldiers of interrupting their careers for temporary assignment to recruiting.

- **Recruiters from traditional military occupations are more productive.**

In deciding whether to increase the proportions of recruiters coming from MOSs such as combat arms or intelligence to increase productivity, the Army should consider the relative opportunity costs of reassigning soldiers with different MOSs.

- **Empirical results suggest a possible disadvantage of private contracting.**

Contractors used for recruiting are likely to be older, retired military personnel whom young prospects are less likely to trust or relate to as role models. Of course, this cost may be balanced by other benefits.

Recruiter Assignment

- **Recruiters who are similar to the population in their stations' market areas are more successful.**

USAREC, brigades, battalions, and companies might consider innovative approaches to improving this matching. For example, it may be sensible to assign recruiters to especially appropriate stations a month or two before an opening is expected to occur or to delay assignment of some new recruiters for a month or two until an especially appropriate slot opens up.

- **Recruiters assigned to their home states are more productive.**

Another attractive option, given our results on young recruiters, is to expand programs that enable recent enlistees to help with recruiting at their home-area stations.

Setting Missions to Achieve Equity

- **The awards incentive system may under-reward production of high-quality contracts.**

Recruiters accrue points on a monthly basis for contracts that they and their stations produce. Accrual of specified numbers of points over specified numbers of months lead to command-level awards such as stars, badges, and rings. Discrepancies between the relative costs of and the relative points for signing high- and lower-quality prospects, combined with the availability of station bonus points for recruiters signing any prospects, may induce recruiters to direct too much effort to enlisting lower-quality prospects. Increasing the relative points for high-quality contracts should be considered.

- **Significant inequities exist among markets.**

The substantial variation in the probabilities of success across stations could be lessened through more careful consideration of demographic factors.

- **From an equity perspective, the current treatment of stations with USAR recruiters is problematic.**

Improved coordination of USAR and regular Army missioning could increase both equity and the number of high-quality enlistees.

Setting Missions to Increase Productivity

- **Efficient missioning requires reliance on past performance.**

The lion's share of the potential gains to mission reallocations is due to greater responsiveness of effort to missions in stations that have been more successful recently. In allocating missions, USAREC should consider more heavy reliance on recent past performance, while being careful to avoid strong disincentives for productivity that could result if recruiters perceive that productivity is punished with higher future missions.

- **Production of high-quality enlistments might be increased by increasing total missions, but there are limits and pitfalls.**

In considering increases in aggregate high-quality missions, the following should be kept in mind: (a) the marginal impacts of increasing aggregate missions diminish as missions increase, (b) increased short-run productivity may come at a long-run cost because only a fraction of the extra contracts missioned would actually be attained, and most importantly, (c) the difficulty of recruiting has changed dramatically since 2003, and as a result, higher missions may be unachievable today; if so, raising them could prove counterproductive.

- **Mission allocations reflecting market quality and recruiter responses can increase high-quality enlistments and save money.**

Productivity improvements achieved by reallocating a fixed total mission could be almost costless. Moreover, if requirements were to increase, productivity improvements resulting from use of a mission allocation scheme based on our econometric model could save substantial resources. For example, every additional 1,000 high-quality recruits gained through better mission allocation could save the Army $6 million if the alternative were to increase enlistments by 1,000 through increases in the number of recruiters.

- **The measure of recent past success we employed in the data analysis has desirable attributes, but alternative measures should be considered.**

The measure we used in the data analysis has the advantages of (a) being implementable in real time, and (b) mitigating incentives to limit production to avoid future mission increases. However, the use of a missioning process that could be viewed as "punishing success," as well as the task of communicating it to the field, raise leadership and morale issues that we haven't analyzed.

- **The addition of DEP losses to missions to create performance goals did not undermine productivity during 2001 to 2003, but this policy should be reviewed.**

USAREC cannot accurately predict stations' DEP losses that will occur during future months for which USAREC must determine missions. If missions are allocated optimally (i.e., to maximize expected contracts at the command level), then adding DEP losses to station goals (the current practice)—which deviates from the optimal missions—will tend to decrease high-quality enlistments. USAREC should consider other approaches to limiting DEP losses that are not directly connected to the missioning, points accrual, and awards processes. For example, USAREC might consider a policy of providing special recognition for stations that have unusually low DEP-loss rates or innovative DEP-management programs.

- **A large portion of the short-term variation in enlistments is due to randomness.**

Much of the monthly variation in contracts is due to chance events that average out of the course of a few months. This suggests that missions might be specified as applying to longer time intervals than a single month (e.g., a quarter).

Promotion Prospects and Incentives for Recruiting

- **On average, becoming a recruiter increases promotion rates.**

We have been told by many personnel at USAREC and by recruiters in the field that there is a widespread view among noncommissioned officers (NCOs) that being assigned to recruiting is a "career killer" because it worsens promotion prospects. The leading concern in this regard appears to be the detrimental effects on future promotion prospects of interrupting a soldier's career in his or her primary MOS. Our data analyses indicate, however, that serving as a recruiter *improved* promotion prospects. Spreading the word could increase rates of volunteering for recruiting and help maintain the morale of recruiters.

- **Recruiters whose stations perform well relative to other stations are promoted faster.**

We cannot judge whether the magnitudes of the rewards for successful recruiting are at appropriate levels, but it is clear that there is a significant incentive in the form of improved promotion prospects for recruiters to be productive.

Identifying and Dealing with Unproductive Recruiters

- The Army appears to be using a sound management policy of replacing, but not punishing, new recruiters who are consistently unproductive.

Large proportions of recruiters who consistently underproduce during the first several months of their tours might not deserve negative personnel actions. It might make sense to replace them, nonetheless. It appears that the Army is applying sound management practices by returning unproductive new recruiters to their primary MOSs and not slowing their career progressions in those occupations.

Acknowledgments

Many people have helped us by providing information, advice, and assistance. We are indebted to more U.S. Army personnel than we can name individually. However, Rod Lunger, from the United States Army Recruiting Command, was especially helpful in providing data on multiple occasions. We thank George Sheldon of the Veteran's Administration for providing special tabulations of veteran populations by state. We also thank RAND colleagues John Adams for very helpful statistical advice and Bruce Orvis and Ellen Pint for valuable input. Jan Hanley, Jennifer Pace, and Stephanie Williamson of RAND provided extensive expert assistance in obtaining, cleaning, and processing data. Michael Woodward and Nancy Good helped immensely in the preparation of the manuscript. Jim Hosek and John Romley of RAND provided very thoughtful and constructive technical reviews that helped us improve this report in many ways.

Acronyms

79R	Career recruiter ("79 Romeo")
AFQT	Armed Forces Qualification Test
ARISS-MPA	Army Recruiting Information Support System—Mission Production Awards
CMF	Career Management Field
DA	Department of the Army
DEP	Delayed Entry Program
DoD	Department of Defense
EMF	Enlisted Master File
E-4	Specialist/Corporal
E-5	Sergeant
E-6	Staff Sergeant
E-7	Sergeant First Class
FY	Fiscal Year
HQ	High Quality
MOS	Military Occupational Specialty
NCO	Noncommissioned Officer
NPS	Non Prior Service

OPRA	On-Production, Regular Army [recruiter]
QMA	Qualified Military Available
RA	Regular Army
USAR	U.S. Army Reserve
USAREC	U.S. Army Recruiting Command

CHAPTER ONE

Introduction

On a continuing basis, the U.S. Army Recruiting Command (USAREC) is faced with the challenge of ensuring that the flow of qualified volunteers is adequate to meet future active-duty accession requirements. Success in meeting this objective is highly dependent on several elements of the overall recruiting system. The key elements of this system are highlighted in Figure 1.1. Some of these elements are largely beyond the Recruiting Command's control. For example, manpower or end-strength requirements determined outside of USAREC

Figure 1.1
Key Elements of the Recruiting "System"

Contract Mission (Demand factors)	**Market Quality** (Supply factors)
Volume requirement *Quality composition* *Term of service* *Occupational and gender mix*	*Market demographics* *Educational opportunities* *Youth labor market* *Propensity*
Recruiting Resources (Policy instruments)	**Recruiter Management** (Human resource management)
Educational benefits *Bonuses and military pay* *Recruiters* *Advertising*	*Recruiter selection and training* *Recruiter assignment* *Missions and performance measurement* *Incentives and career management*

RAND *MG433-1.1*

determine the monthly contract or enlistment mission (demand) as well as its composition. Also important are supply factors traditionally considered in recruiting studies, such as market demographics, alternative labor market and educational opportunities, and prevailing attitudes regarding military service.

Whatever the prevailing supply and demand conditions, policymakers have several options for increasing the flow of enlistment contracts. Most manpower research has focused on the role of recruiting resources, such as military pay, enlistment benefits, advertising programs, or numbers of recruiters. Although such policy instruments have demonstrable enlistment-expansion effects, they can be quite costly to use.[1]

In contrast, there has been little research on a range of human resource management policies that may enhance the productivity of the recruiting force. Such policies include personnel selection and training, recruiter assignment, performance measurement, and the design of incentive systems that motivate recruiters to be more productive. The lack of information on the effectiveness of these recruiter-management options is unfortunate because more effective policies could increase enlistments for little, if any, additional resources.

This report documents research designed to reduce this knowledge gap and provide new insights to help guide future recruiter-management policies. Based on econometric analyses of three large and detailed datasets, this research provides new evidence concerning alternative policies and their likely impacts on recruiting outcomes.

Background

In this report we present and discuss empirical findings relevant to recruiter-management policies in four broad areas: (a) selecting soldiers for recruiting duty, (b) assigning recruiters to stations, the Army's ver-

---

[1]   As a recent example, Dertouzos and Garber (2003) provide marginal cost estimates of increasing high-quality enlistments via expansions in military pay, the recruiting force, or advertising. These costs range between $13,000 and $60,000 per additional high-quality recruit.

sion of sales offices, (c) setting missions, the Army's version of sales quotas, and (d) using promotion policy to enhance recruiter productivity. In this chapter we provide background and context for the analyses that follow, emphasizing the years 1998 through 2003, the time period on which our data analyses are focused. In providing this background, we paint with a broad brush for two reasons. First, many of the issues are complex, but the details are not important for our purposes. Second, during the time periods covered by our data, various institutions, policies, and procedures changed in ways that have not been thoroughly documented.[2]

Our analyses focus on recruiting of enlisted personnel (i.e., not commissioned officers) for active duty (i.e., not reserve duty). Soldiers on active duty are commonly referred to as members of the "regular Army" (RA). The activities of "on-production, regular Army" (OPRA) recruiters are focused on convincing prospects to sign enlistment contracts or to "enlist." OPRA recruiters, and in most instances their supervisors or "station commanders," work out of recruiting stations scattered around the country. Stations are the most disaggregated unit of the Recruiting Command within a hierarchical organization summarized in Table 1.1. Each recruiting station is assigned a sales territory

Table 1.1
Organization of U.S. Army Recruiting Command
Within Lower 48 States

Unit	Number as of June 2000
Brigade	5
Battalion	41
Company	243
Station	1,656
OPRA recruiters	6,261

SOURCE: "Manning the Army of the Future, PAE Recruiting Update," USAREC (no date, received August 2000).

---

[2] Much of the information presented here is based on several face-to-face interviews at USAREC in August 2000 and April 2003. We have also collected information from USAREC and U.S. Army Personnel Command (PERSCOM) staff by telephone and email, reviewed many internal USAREC memos and briefings, and conducted face-to-face interviews with recruiters from several stations.

or market area defining the prospects whom they may enlist, comprised of students in high schools and colleges assigned to each station and places of residence for prospects who are not in school.

Recruiting activity is generally focused on individuals 17 to 21 years old who have not previously served in the military (non-prior-service or NPS), with an emphasis on males. For example, in fiscal year 1998 (FY98), 82 percent of enlistees were male. An enlistment contract specifies the job field or "military occupational specialty" (MOS) for which the enlistee will be trained and a date on which the enlistee is to report for duty, which is generally referred to as a "shipping" or "accession" date.[3] Prospects may sign contracts that involve shipping dates several months in the future, in which case they enter the Delayed Entry Program (DEP).[4] Enlistees who change their minds about joining the Army and drop out of the DEP are referred to as "DEP losses." Losses from the DEP are not uncommon,[5] and reducing DEP loss rates is an important objective of the Recruiting Command.

The U.S. Army's recruiting force is made up of relatively experienced soldiers—typically, at rank E-5 (sergeant)—who are reassigned from their primary MOSs to temporary duty as recruiters, typically for three years. Recruiters who want to complete their Army careers in recruiting can state this preference during the second year of their initial assignment, and those who are accepted as career recruiters are reassigned to MOS 79R ("79 Romeos").[6] After completing their initial terms in recruiting, other soldiers return to the "mainstream Army" and resume their careers in their original or primary MOSs.

---

[3] In addition to recruiters, job counselors also play an important role in the Army enlistment process; see Asch and Karoly (1993), who write (p. xi) "While the recruiter's job is to sell the idea of military service to applicants, the counselor's job is to sell the contract—the military occupation (or occupation group), the enlistment term, the accession date, and the enlistment incentive package, if available."

[4] Sometimes delayed entry is required by the circumstances of the enlistee (e.g., a high school senior who must wait to graduate), at other times entry is delayed until a training slot will be open for the enlistee's MOS, or to suit the preferences of the prospect.

[5] For example, in our data from January 2001 through June 2003, about 15 percent of the "high-quality" prospects (see below) who sign contracts become DEP losses.

[6] USAREC has a target of roughly 10 percent of recruiters to become 79Rs.

Some soldiers volunteer for recruiting duty, and others are assigned to recruiting without having volunteered.[7] The latter recruiters are referred to as "DA (Department of the Army) selected." The processes for nominating soldiers for recruiting became more centralized during our data period, but generally, soldiers are nominated for recruiting duty if they are regarded as good performers based on observation by superiors or review of written performance evaluations. All nominees (both volunteers and DA-selected) are screened to identify those who are disqualified from recruiting for any of several reasons such as physical, financial, legal, or family difficulties.

Many DA-selected recruiters indicate they were far from enthusiastic about being assigned to recruiting duty. One reason is that many of them are satisfied with their mainstream Army careers (primary MOS, rate of promotion). In addition, recruiting duty often involves difficult goals, very long hours, lack of predictable time off, and considerable stress. Moreover, roughly two-thirds of recruiters live more than 50 miles from the nearest military installation, which makes it difficult to benefit from on-base housing, shopping, and healthcare. But perhaps most important, there is a widespread belief among soldiers that unproductive recruiters are likely to receive negative performance reviews, which would be "career killers" in terms of future promotion prospects.

Once a soldier is trained for recruiting duty, he or she is assigned to a recruiting station.[8] USAREC assigns each recruiter to a brigade and makes a recommendation about the battalion to which the recruiter will be assigned. In making assignments to brigades, a primary objective of USAREC is to equalize across brigades the ratio of recruiters assigned ("faces") to recruiters authorized ("spaces"). The number of authorizations is based on analyses done at USAREC of the aggregate potential of each brigade's assigned market areas. In addition, USAREC tries to assign recruiters to one of the battalions they most

---

[7] As of mid-2000, roughly one-third of current recruiters had volunteered for recruiting duty.

[8] Once assigned to a station for an initial tour as a recruiter, recruiters are rarely transferred to another station during this initial tour.

prefer. For example, in FY00 roughly 84 percent of volunteers and 58 percent of DA-selected recruiters were assigned to one of their three most preferred battalions. Once recruiters are assigned to battalions, battalions assign recruiters to companies and make recommendations about assignments to stations. At USAREC, interviewees report that very little is known about how assignments and recommendations are determined below the command level, and the widespread view is that different battalions and companies do this in various ways that defy generalization.

Monthly contract missions for three categories of prospects, often referred to simply as "missions," are the Army's version of sales quotas. Recruiting success in any month, commonly referred to as "making mission" or "boxing," is defined as meeting or exceeding the number of contracts or enlistments missioned category by category (including possible adjustments based on substitution rules described below). National- or command-level contract missions derive from national accession missions—i.e., the number of enlistees in various occupational categories needed to report for training during particular time periods—that are assigned to USAREC.[9] Contract missions are determined separately for three categories of regular Army enlistees. One of these categories is high school seniors falling into Armed Forces Qualification Test (AFQT) categories I through IIIA, which corresponds to the top half of the AFQT distribution. Such enlistees are often referred to as "senior alphas" or "high-quality" seniors. The second category is NPS high school graduates in AFQT test categories I through IIIA ("grad alphas" or "high-quality grads"). The third category is all "others" (test score categories below IIIA, not high school graduates, prior service).

National-level contract missions for each month are assigned or allocated by USAREC to brigades with recommendations about how brigade missions should be allocated to battalions.[10] Battalions then

---

[9] Accession missions are determined on the basis of target Army end-strength and the availability of training slots.

[10] While separate missions are assigned for each month, they are determined and conveyed for three months or a quarter of the year at a time.

allocate their missions to companies with recommendations about allocations to individual recruiting stations.

Over the course of our data period (1998 through 2003), various changes were made in USAREC procedures and models used to determine missions for brigades and recommendations for battalions. A major objective of many of these changes was to align missions more closely with the aggregate market potential of the stations within each battalion. These attempts reflect a widespread belief within USAREC that many stations could produce more high-quality contracts, but fail to do so because their missions are too low given the quality of their markets.[11]

During the early part of our data period, each station's missions were formally assigned to individual OPRA recruiters within the station, and success and rewards were determined on an individual basis. Beginning in FY00, stations in two brigades[12] were missioned and evaluated on a team or station basis, and in FY01 the remaining three brigades were converted to station missioning. All stations remained on station missioning beyond June 2003, the last month for which we analyze data.

Under both individual and station missioning, recruiters earn prespecified points for each enlistment in different categories and bonus points for succeeding in making mission or "boxing."[13] Accrual of specified numbers of points over the course of specified numbers of months leads to command-level awards such as stars, badges, and

---

[11] In the analysis reported in Chapter Four, we develop econometric estimates of the relative market potentials or quality of stations' recruiting areas. In that chapter we describe how USAREC incorporated market factors in models used to determine brigade and battalion missions.

[12] Brigades 1 and 2, located in the northeastern and southeastern United States, were the two early adopters of station missioning.

[13] At various times, additional points have been awarded when an enlistee in the DEP shipped or when an enlistee successfully completed basic training. In addition, at various times under station missioning, bonus points have been awarded to boxing stations and stations that met their missioned "volumes" (achieved at least as many enlistments as were missioned, but didn't box) if their companies, battalions, and brigades succeeded.

rings.[14] Although recruiters find it important to earn such rewards,[15] they are perhaps even more motivated to succeed in achieving whatever goals are assigned to them, and the most tangible measure of success for recruiters is the achievement of their individual or station missions.[16]

To make mission, the individual or station must enlist at least as many prospects in each of the three categories as the mission assigned plus any DEP losses formally recorded in that category in that month,[17] after applying substitution rules that can change from month to month.[18] Roughly 57 percent of recruiting stations include U.S. Army Reserve (USAR) recruiters, and for such a station to succeed—i.e., achieve or make its monthly missions—and recruiters to be eligible for bonus points, the station must make *both* its RA and USAR missions. Finally, under station missioning, a recruiter must sign at least one prospect during a month in order to receive any bonus points based on the station's (company's, battalion's, or brigade's) performance in that month.

---

[14] For detailed information about awards and required numbers of points to achieve each step, see Oken and Asch (1997).

[15] For example, we have been told that recruiters generally feel that for a recruiting tour to be viewed as successful, the recruiter should achieve at least a gold badge.

[16] Recruiters are also evaluated by their station commanders and other superiors using a form known as the NCO Evaluation Report, which assesses performance along many dimensions, such as competence, physical fitness and military bearing, leadership, and responsibility and accountability.

[17] Stations appear to have little, if any, control over the month in which a DEP loss is formally recorded and, thus, the month in which the station's mission in that category is in effect increased. The process is as follows. Once it becomes clear that an enlistee in the DEP is determined to break his or her contract and cannot be convinced to ship (report for duty), the recruiting station fills out a Request for Separation form, which is forwarded to the battalion. The DEP loss is formally recorded during the month in which the battalion signs off on this request.

[18] In recent years, contracts for grad alphas usually were allowed to substitute for contracts for senior alphas or others, and contracts for senior alphas usually were allowed to substitute for contracts for others.

Organization of the Report

The remainder of the report is organized as follows. In Chapter Two, we relate the productivity of individual OPRA recruiters to their personal attributes and the characteristics of the markets in which they work, and discuss implications for recruiter selection and assignment. In Chapter Three, we present descriptive analyses of recruiting stations' recent success in achieving their regular Army missions. These results are useful in evaluating whether recent missions represent equitable performance standards. In Chapter Four, we develop and estimate a model of station productivity and establish empirical links between station-level high-quality enlistments and a large set of explanatory variables, including missions, DEP losses, market characteristics, and other determinants of the productivity of recruiter effort. Based on these results, we assess alternative missioning approaches in Chapter Five. In Chapter Six, we document our third empirical analysis, which examines promotion rates of recruiters and compares them with cohorts who have taken different career paths. In our concluding Chapter Seven, we integrate our findings and discuss implications for the design of more effective recruiter-management policies.

CHAPTER TWO

Determinants of Individual Recruiter Productivity

In this chapter we examine recruiter-level productivity and link enlistment outcomes to a host of factors, including local market characteristics, individual recruiter attributes, and several variables of potential policy interest. Based on this analysis, we draw inferences for a variety of human resource policies, including selection of recruiters, assignment of individuals to stations, and setting performance targets or missions. We begin with a description of the dataset.

Individual Recruiter Data

For this study, USAREC provided us with an administrative file[1] that contained information on the missions and number of contracts signed by individual recruiters during FY98 through FY00. We analyzed the data for recruiters with individual missions, which included all recruiters in FY98 and FY99 and recruiters in three brigades in FY00. We also deleted records of recruiters who were not fully "on production," such as station commanders. The resulting analysis file contained 131,063 records (recruiter-month pairs) for 10,136 OPRA recruiters.

The variables used in this analysis are described in Table 2.1, along with their sample mean values and standard deviations.[2] We analyzed monthly production by individual recruiters of high-quality and

---

[1] The file is called the Army Recruiting Information Support System—Mission Production Awards (ARISS-MPA).

[2] Appendix C provides more detailed information about these data.

total contracts. Over this time period, on average recruiters enlisted less than one high-quality prospect per month (mean = 0.6815). This average level of production fell short of the typical recruiting goal: the high-quality mission[3] plus losses from DEP (mean = 1.2242).[4] We also gathered contract and mission information for the recruiter's assigned recruiting station.

Table 2.1
Individual Recruiter Data, 1998–2000

Variable	Definition	Mean	Standard Deviation
DEPENDENT VARIABLES (enlistment counts):			
High-quality grads and seniors		0.6815	0.8239
Total contracts		1.3295	1.1784
Station high-quality contracts		2.0005	1.9325
INDEPENDENT VARIABLES			
Mission variables:			
High-quality goal (mission plus DEP losses)		1.2242	0.7326
Total mission (excluding DEP losses)		1.6536	0.8325
Station high-quality mission		5.5066	2.2660
Station size indicator variables:			
R2	Station has 2 recruiters (0,1)	0.0994	0.2992
R3	Station has 3 recruiters (0,1)	0.1679	0.3738

[3] Missions for individual recruiters can differ from month to month very substantially in relative terms, since missions must take integer values. For example, a recruiter who had a total mission of one in a particular month frequently had a mission of two enlistments during the next month.

[4] In signing a contract, enlistees commit to an accession or "ship" date that can be almost immediate or several months in the future. For purposes of performance measurement, any person who drops out of the DEP before accessing is counted against production during the month the DEP loss is officially recorded and is, therefore, equivalent to an increase in that month's mission. We examine the implications of this approach in Chapters Four and Five.

Table 2.1—continued

Variable	Definition	Mean	Standard Deviation
R4	Station has 4 recruiters (0,1)	0.2181	0.4130
R5	Station has 5 recruiters (0,1)	0.2188	0.4134
R6	Station has more than 5 recruiters (0,1)	0.2731	0.4455
Month and year indicator variables:			
M2	October	0.0814	0.2734
M3	November	0.0836	0.2768
M4	December	0.0813	0.2733
M5	January	0.0811	0.2729
M6	February	0.0859	0.2803
M7	March	0.0860	0.2804
M8	April	0.0874	0.2824
M9	May	0.0875	0.2826
M10	June	0.0805	0.2721
M11	July	0.0819	0.2741
M12	August	0.0836	0.2768
Y99	Fiscal year 1999	0.3823	0.4860
Y00	Fiscal year 2000	0.1881	0.3908
Region of country variables:			
Mountain	Station in Mountain state	0.0490	0.2159
North Central	Station in North Central state	0.2155	0.4112
South	Station in Southern state	0.4540	0.4979
Pacific	Station in Pacific state	0.0878	0.2830
Market variables:			
QMA	Qualified Military Available per recruiter	566.99	425.86
Unemployment	Log (unemployment rate)	1.4271	0.4165
Wage	Log (military/civilian wage rate)	−4.5587	0.1286
College Enrollment	Fraction of youth enrolled in college	0.4143	0.0543
Competition	Army market share 1999 (percent)	38.0249	7.9527

Table 2.1—continued

Variable	Definition	Mean	Standard Deviation
Demographic variables:			
Vet pop < 32	Veteran population under 32*	0.2168	0.0608
Vet pop 33–42	Veteran population 33–42*	0.3889	0.1282
Vet pop 43–55	Veteran population 43–55*	0.8551	0.2411
Vet pop 56–65	Veteran population 56–65*	0.5748	0.1665
Vet pop 66–72	Veteran population 66–72*	0.4669	0.1494
Vet pop 73+	Veteran population 73 and older [A]	0.5681	0.2396
Black population	Proportion of station area	0.1419	0.1415
Hispanic population	Proportion of station area	0.1493	0.2018
Recruiter characteristics:			
Black	African American recruiter (0,1)	0.3394	0.4735
Hispanic	Hispanic recruiter (0,1)	0.0601	0.2376
Other race	Other race (0,1)	0.0712	0.2571
Cat I–II	AFQT category I or II	0.3630	0.4809
Cat IIIA	AFQT category IIIA	0.2543	0.4355
Cat IIIB	AFQT category IIIB	0.2995	0.4580
High school	High school graduate, no college	0.4697	0.4991
College	Attended college	0.5249	0.4994
Single	Not currently married	0.1169	0.3213
Dependents	At least one dependent	0.6991	0.4587
Female	Female	0.0663	0.2489
Young	Age under 30 years	0.2496	0.4328
Older	Age over 35 years	0.1865	0.3895
Military Occupational Specialties (MOSs)			
Technical	Technical occupations (Specialties: 31, 33, 35, 51, 54, 63, 67, 77, 74, 81, 27, 62, 68, 52)**	0.2413	0.4278
Intel	Military intelligence (Specialties: 25, 96, 98)	0.0104	0.1014

Table 2.1—continued

Variable	Definition	Mean	Standard Deviation
Combat	Combat (Artillery, Infantry, etc.) (Specialties: 11, 12, 13, 14, 18, 19, 82, 23)	0.3722	0.4834
Logistics	Logistics (Specialties: 55, 88, 92)	0.1186	0.3233
Other	All other specialties	0.1720	0.3774
Career recruiter	79 Romeo	0.0898	0.2859
Home state indicator	Station located in home state (0,1)	0.2684	0.4431
Interaction variables:	**Interactions of recruiter characteristics and population**		
Black*Black Population	Black indicator variable multiplied by black population variable	0.0733	0.1365
Hispanic*Hispanic Population	Hispanic indicator variable multiplied by Hispanic population	0.0195	0.1042
College*College Enrollment	Some college indicator variable multiplied by college enrollment variable	0.2170	0.2105

*Divided by population of 17- to 21-year-old males.

**The occupational specialties included by category are detailed in Appendix C.

We then linked production data with a variety of station and market variables described in Table 2.1. Information was gathered on the number of recruiters assigned to the station, the month of production, the fiscal year, and the region of the country. A variety of economic and demographic variables were also collected. It is important to note that these measures pertain to various dimensions of the quality of the market assigned to the station, which often includes multiple recruiters who are typically responsible for specific parts of the "sales territory," for example, individual high schools. Market data included the number of "qualified military available" youth (QMA),[5] the local unemployment

---

[5] QMA counts net out from youth population totals the estimated numbers of youth in college and those who are ineligible for military service for physical reasons or because of criminal records.

rate and its monthly change, a measure of the relative military-to-civilian wage rate, and college enrollment. Other demographic information included local veteran populations (in age categories), and both Hispanic and African American populations, expressed as proportions of the total population within the station's market boundaries. The 1999 Army share of total active-duty military enlistments in the station's area was included to control for competition from other services.[6]

In addition to market descriptions, information was gathered on a broad range of personal characteristics of recruiters. These included race, AFQT categories, education, marital status, gender, and age. Dichotomous variables representing broad groups of occupational specialties were created. Other dummy variables in the dataset indicate whether the individual was a career recruiter (79 Romeo) or was assigned to a station located in the same state where he or she lived when enlisting in the Army. Finally, three interaction variables were computed to test the proposition that recruiters with particular characteristics are more productive if these characteristics are more common in their local markets. For example, one might expect that a recruiter with college experience would be more effective in dealing with college students than a recruiter with only a high school education.

Regression Results

The links between individual contract production and the aforementioned market and personal characteristics were examined using two different multiple-regression techniques. In Table 2.2, we report coefficients and standard errors for a linear model of monthly production for high-quality and total enlistments. In general, the estimated effects were statistically significant and, in cases where there were theoretical expectations or previous research results, consistent with expectations. To test the robustness of the results with respect to an alternative func-

---

[6]   For about 25 percent of the local markets, Army share data were not available. The missing data were replaced with predictions derived from a regression of Army shares on the full set of explanatory variables. This regression is reported in Appendix A, Table A.1.

tional form, we also analyzed a logistic model where the ordered values of the dependent variable were zero, 1, 2, or 3 or more high-quality contracts. These results, which were virtually identical, are reported in Appendix A, Table A.2.

Table 2.2
Individual Recruiter Production: Linear Regression Results, 1998–2000

Variable	High-Quality Contracts		All Contracts	
	Coefficient	Standard Error	Coefficient	Standard Error
Intercept	−0.3908	0.1099	−1.5657	0.1510
Mission*	0.1121	0.0031	0.1273	0.0039
2-recruiter station	−0.0322	0.0173	−0.0815	0.0238
3-recruiter station	−0.0493	0.0169	−0.1132	0.0232
4-recruiter station	−0.0782	0.0169	−0.1694	0.0232
5-recruiter station	−0.0798	0.0172	−0.1829	0.0236
6-plus recruiter station	−0.0945	0.0175	−0.2325	0.0240
October	−0.0297	0.0111	−0.0314	0.0153
November	0.0583	0.0111	0.0555	0.0152
December	−0.0891	0.0112	−0.1870	0.0154
January	−0.0645	0.0112	−0.2464	0.0154
February	0.1250	0.0110	0.0588	0.0151
March	0.0475	0.0110	−0.0148	0.0151
April	0.1262	0.0110	0.0918	0.0151
May	0.0643	0.0112	0.1547	0.0154
June	0.0021	0.0113	−0.0644	0.0155
July	0.0134	0.0112	−0.0967	0.0154
August	0.0214	0.0112	−0.1169	0.0154
Fiscal year 1999	−0.0512	0.0054	0.0635	0.0074
Fiscal year 2000	0.0201	0.0075	0.1890	0.0102
Mountain region	0.0113	0.0119	0.0268	0.0164
North Central region	−0.0126	0.0078	−0.0256	0.0108
South region	−0.0128	0.0071	−0.0151	0.0097
Pacific region	0.0016	0.0099	0.0065	0.0136
QMA per recruiter	0.00004	0.00001	0.00003	0.00001
Log(unemployment)	0.0186	0.0067	0.1130	0.0091

Table 2.2—continued

| Variable | High-Quality Contracts | | All Contracts | |
	Coefficient	Standard Error	Coefficient	Standard Error
Log (civilian/military wage)	−0.1444	0.0203	−0.4146	0.0279
College population	−0.0033	0.0006	−0.0034	0.0009
Vet pop < 33	−0.1045	0.0780	0.3787	0.1072
Vet pop 33–42	0.1389	0.0558	0.0960	0.0767
Vet pop 43–55	0.0146	0.0356	−0.0389	0.0490
Vet pop 56–65	0.0285	0.0578	0.1619	0.0794
Vet pop 65–72	0.1857	0.0699	−0.2152	0.0961
Vet pop 73+	0.0719	0.0297	0.0036	0.0408
Army market share 1999	0.0102	0.0003	0.0178	0.0004
Black population	−0.0885	0.0267	0.3421	0.0367
Hispanic population	0.0995	0.0153	0.2311	0.0211
Recruiter characteristics:				
Cat I-II	−0.0079	0.0095	−0.0410	0.0130
Cat IIIA	−0.0007	0.0095	−0.0256	0.0131
Cat IIIB	0.0122	0.0091	0.0028	0.0125
High school grad, no college	−0.0136	0.0337	−0.0327	0.0463
Attended college	0.0220	0.0483	0.0277	0.0663
Black recruiter	−0.0446	0.0083	−0.0001	0.0115
Hispanic recruiter	0.0214	0.0188	0.0617	0.0258
Other race	−0.0347	0.0101	0.0084	0.0138
Single	−0.0143	0.0085	−0.0549	0.0116
Dependents	0.0222	0.0060	0.0327	0.0082
Female	−0.0251	0.0097	−0.0140	0.0133
Young	0.0425	0.0057	0.0472	0.0078
Older	−0.0461	0.0062	−0.0843	0.0085
Technical	0.0319	0.0076	0.0601	0.0105
Intel	0.0789	0.0226	0.0336	0.0311
Combat	0.0446	0.0083	0.0806	0.0113
Other	0.0211	0.0073	0.0546	0.0100
Career recruiter	−0.1305	0.0094	−0.2632	0.0129
Home state	0.0237	0.0052	0.0306	0.0071

Table 2.2—continued

Variable	High-Quality Contracts		All Contracts	
	Coefficient	Standard Error	Coefficient	Standard Error
Interactions:				
Black rec*Black Pop	0.0853	0.0348	0.2200	0.0478
Hispanic rec*Hisp Pop	−0.1673	0.0407	−0.1251	0.0559
College rec*College Pop	0.0002	0.0008	0.0005	0.0011
R-squared	.0389		.0656	

*Mission was defined as high-quality mission for the first model, total mission for the second model.

For example, it is believed that when missions are higher (other things equal), recruiters work harder, and as a result produce more contracts.[7] The estimates suggest that, on average, a one-unit increase in the high-quality mission leads to a 0.112 increase in the average number of high-quality contracts written in the same month. Using the logistic model results reported in Appendix A, Table A.2, one can calculate predicted probability distributions of contracts for different levels of missions, holding other factors in the model constant. These distributions are presented in Table 2.3. With a monthly mission of one high-quality enlistment, about 50 percent of recruiters would fail to write a single high-quality contract, a little over 35 percent would make the mission exactly, and nearly 15 percent would exceed their mission. All things equal, the addition of another high-quality mission would increase the failure rate to about 82 percent.[8]

Returning to Table 2.2, one finds systematic variation in the average productivity of recruiters depending on station size. Even controlling for mission, larger stations have lower average productivity, after accounting for systematic differences in market characteristics. For

---

[7] In an early example, Polich, Dertouzos, and Press (1986) report an average enlistment elasticity of 0.27 with respect to mission. The implied elasticity from the estimates reported in Table 2.2 is 0.20.

[8] In particular, if the high-quality mission were equal to two, then the predicted probability of zero or one contract is 0.4132 + 0.4067 = 0.8199.

Table 2.3
Probability Distributions of High-Quality Contracts for Various High-Quality Mission Levels

	Mission			
	0	1	2	3
Probability of:				
0 high quality	0.5815	0.5021	0.4132	0.3152
1 high quality	0.3004	0.3517	0.4067	0.4641
2 high quality	0.0932	0.1149	0.1409	0.1716
3 high quality	0.0249	0.0313	0.0392	0.0490

example, average recruiter productivity in a station with six or more production recruiters is 14 percent lower than in stations with a single recruiter.[9]

There is also systematic seasonal and year-to-year variation in productivity. Write rates appear to be almost 30 percent higher in spring than they are in December and January. In comparison to FY98, productivity fell in FY99 before rising in FY00.

Not surprisingly, recruiter productivity varies with local market conditions. High-quality enlistments rise with increases in the QMA population per recruiter and the unemployment rate, and fall with higher civilian wages and rates of college attendance.[10] Other categories of enlistments (prior service, lower AFQT categories, and nongraduates) are substantially more responsive to local employment opportunities as reflected in prevailing wages and the unemployment rate.[11]

---

[9] The coefficient of −0.0945 for the dichotomous variable representing six or more recruiters in the high-quality equation is 14 percent of the average high-quality write rate of 0.6815.

[10] The implied estimates of the elasticities of high-quality contracts with respect to the unemployment rate and the civilian wage rate (computed at the mean values of the independent variables) are 0.027 and 0.212, respectively.

[11] The much lower estimated elasticities of high-quality contracts with respect to wages and unemployment compared with those for total contracts is likely to reflect major differences between high-quality and other prospects in terms of their best alternatives to military service and, accordingly, how they view the military-service option. In particular, relatively high proportions of high-quality prospects are likely to view college as their best alternative to military service and, accordingly, find military service attractive because it provides a means of financing a college education. In contrast, relatively high proportions of other

Market demographics also play significant roles. The presence of veterans is important, but the impact depends on the age distribution of those with past military service. In addition, the impacts of veterans vary across the two categories of contracts. For example, the presence of young veterans (age less than 33) appears to be negatively related to production of high-quality contracts (although this result is not statistically significant), while the impact on total contracts is positive and significant. The presence of more veterans between the ages of 33 and 42 has a substantial positive coefficient in the equation for the number of high-quality contracts. In contrast, more veterans between ages 65 and 72 have the opposite effect. The pattern of estimated effects of veteran populations of different age groups is difficult to rationalize.

Several individual recruiter characteristics are also important in determining outcomes. Younger male recruiters with dependents are more productive. Career recruiters and those over 35 years of age have lower productivity rates, other things equal. Productivity also varies by primary occupational specialty. Compared to the benchmark (omitted category) logistics occupation, personnel with primary MOSs in technical, military intelligence, and combat arms areas have significantly higher productivity. On the other hand, a recruiter's education level and AFQT category appear not to matter.

Recruiters' races and genders also matter, but the relationships are complex. As noted earlier, interaction terms were included to test the proposition that recruiters with specific attributes are more effective when recruiting candidates with similar attributes. The evidence suggests that well-educated recruiters are not more productive in communities with relatively high rates of college attendance. In addition, Hispanic recruiters do not appear to have higher write rates in more heavily Hispanic communities.[12] On the other hand, African American recruiters, while appearing to recruit high-quality prospects less

---

prospects are likely to view employment as their best alternative, and thus view the military as providing a job. As a result, local employment conditions are likely to be much less salient for high-quality prospects than for other prospects.

[12] In fact, if interpreted at face value, the estimates suggest that Hispanic recruiters are more productive on average, but they do less well in Hispanic communities. This could reflect heterogeneity in Hispanic populations and, perhaps, Spanish-speaking recruiters tending to be

successfully on average, can outperform their cohorts in markets with relatively high black populations.

Table 2.4 presents the predicted productivity differences between African American and non-Hispanic white recruiters for both high-quality and total contracts, as a function of the proportion of African Americans in the local population. Note that a representative African American recruiter, when assigned to a market with no African Americans, has an average high-quality write rate that is 6.5 percent less than a non-Hispanic white recruiter, other things equal. For total contracts, productivity of black recruiters is superior, roughly 2.7 percent higher in communities with average proportions of blacks of 15 percent. At the extreme, with populations 100 percent black, high-quality and total contracts are 4.2 percent and 18.0 percent higher, respectively, for African American recruiters.

Female recruiters appear to produce slightly fewer high-quality contracts in an average month, other things equal (Table 2.2). We further examined the role of recruiter gender in a regression analysis detailed in Appendix A, Table A.3. The dependent variable in this regression was the fraction of high-quality enlistees who were women, with a sample average value of 0.2306. The results in Appendix A, Table A.3 indicate that the fraction of high-quality enlistees who are women rises by 0.0693 (to a total of nearly 30 percent) if the recruiter is a female. This implies that although women appear to be less successful

Table 2.4
Comparative Productivity of African American Recruiters: Variations by Racial Composition of Local Market

Black Population	High-Quality Contracts	Total Contracts
0%	−6.5%	0%
15%	−4.7%	2.7%
100%	4.2%	18.0%

NOTE: Percentage differences are for predicted contracts for African American recruiters minus predicted contracts for non-Hispanic white recruiters.

assigned to areas with unobserved market attributes that have negative impacts on recruiting (such as English literacy rates).

at recruiting males, they typically recruit more females, averaging about 23 percent more women than their male counterparts.[13]

During the 1998–2000 period, approximately 27 percent of all recruiters were assigned to stations located in their home state, and if not located in the same state, recruiters were still more likely to be located in states in the same region as their home states. Table 2.5 illustrates this assignment pattern. The first column of numbers reports the percentages of recruiters who were recruited from each of the five regions of the contiguous 48 states. The last five columns report the percentage of recruiters who are assigned to recruiting stations within the region indicated by the column heading who were recruited from the region indicated in the first column of the table. For example, the first row indicates that of recruiters who were assigned to recruiting stations in the Mountain region, 29.6 percent were from that region; for recruiters assigned to stations in the North Central region, only 5.0 percent were from the Mountain region, etc.

Table 2.5
Recruiter Assignments and Home Region

Recruiter Home Region	% Recruiters from Region	Percentage of Recruiters Assigned to Station in:*				
		Mountain	North Central	Northeast	Pacific	South
Mountain	6.1%	29.6%	5.0%	4.4%	9.8%	4.3%
North Central	21.2%	12.8%	53.2%	8.8%	11.5%	14.6%
Northeast	15.6%	7.5%	7.4%	48.0%	7.4%	12.4%
Pacific	11.8%	23.2%	6.7%	6.5%	45.6%	8.3%
South	39.5%	18.9%	24.2%	26.5%	18.0%	55.9%

*Column totals sum to less than 100 percent because some recruiters are assigned to recruiting duty outside the 48 contiguous states.

---

[13] The recruiting of females also appears to be higher in African American communities, especially by nonwhite recruiters. This may partially reflect gender differences in African American youth that result in more women being eligible or inclined toward military service. However, it could be that the relative effectiveness of black recruiters in diverse communities is partially attributable to gender. In other words, black recruiters may be successful in some communities because they are women, not because they are black. In future work, we hope to disentangle the separate impacts of gender and race in reaching diverse populations.

As can be seen in the diagonal elements of the matrix comprised of the last five columns of Table 2.5 (which are shown in bold type), in each region the percentage of recruiters from that region exceeds by a wide margin the percentage of recruiters from that region in the population of all recruiters. For example, only 6.1 percent of all recruiters were from the Mountain region, but nearly 30 percent of the recruiters located in the Mountain region were originally from there. Similar patterns are evident for the other regions. The regression results reported in Table 2.1 suggest that such recruiter assignment is effective. Productivity of recruiters assigned to their home state averages about 4 percent higher, other things equal.[14]

Additional Interpretation of Results

Table 2.6 presents measures of the joint importance of groups or classes of explanatory variables defined in Table 2.1 in explaining high-quality enlistments.[15] For example, differences in predicted contracts due to variations in missions had a standard deviation of 0.0821. Predictions based on market and demographic factors had the largest impact, with a standard deviation of 0.0908. The group of systematic seasonal (calendar month) and fiscal year indicators was next in importance at 0.0699. Regional differences and numbers of recruiters were less important in

---

[14] This productivity gain could understate the efficacy of policies facilitating assignment of recruiters to their home states or regions. For example, to the extent that some recruiters volunteer because of a desire to be closer to home, and volunteers are likely to be assigned to one of their most preferred battalions, the quality and effectiveness of the recruiting force might be improved through higher rates of volunteering.

[15] For each observation, the contribution of a group of variables to explaining predicted contracts was computed by first multiplying the estimated coefficients by the values of the variables within the group and then summing these products over the variables in the group. Second, the (across-observation) standard deviations of these sums were computed and used as measures of importance for the groups of variables. For example, for the pair of variables x_1 and x_2, their contributions for each observation i are $C_i(x_1,x_2) = b_1 x_{i1} + b_2 x_{i2}$, where the b's are the estimated coefficients. The standard deviation across all of the sample observations of the C_i's for each group of variables provides a measure of the importance of that group in explaining observed variations in enlistments.

Table 2.6
Importance of Groups of Variables in Predicting Individual Recruiter Production of High-Quality Contracts

Mean of high-quality contracts	0.6815
Standard deviation of high-quality contracts	0.8239
Standard deviation due to variation in:	
Mission variables	0.0821
Month and year indicators	0.0699
Region of country	0.0073
Market and demographic variables	0.0908
Recruiter characteristics	0.0603
Station size	0.0228

explaining patterns of recruiter productivity in signing high-quality prospects. Finally, all personal characteristics of recruiters jointly have a standard deviation of 0.0603, which indicates that recruiter characteristics included in the regression have about two-thirds the explanatory power of market and demographic factors and about three-fourths of that attributable to missions. This suggests that effective selection and assignment of recruiters could significantly facilitate achievement of monthly production goals at little, if any, cost.

It is important to note that even when one ignores the correlations between prediction components, the sum of all the individual contributions (0.3322) amounts to only a fraction of the standard deviation of high-quality contracts (0.8239). Indeed, the individual recruiter models account for only about 3.9 and 6.6 percent of the observed variation in high-quality and total contracts, respectively. Thus, the individual production model does not explain very much of the month-to-month variation in productivity by individual recruiters.

To some extent, this result is not surprising given that the outcome variable is discrete and concentrated on a few values, with 97 percent being either zero, one, or two contracts. This being the case, it is likely that the model would perform substantially better on data aggregated over several months, several recruiters, or both. To examine this proposition, we summed actual and predicted contracts over three months to see whether we could eliminate much of the random component. We also estimated a station-level model. The coefficient estimates and standard errors for the station-level model are reported in Appendix A, Table A.4.[16]

A summary of the explanatory power of alternative specifications is presented in Table 2.7, relying on R-squared statistics, which measure the proportion of the sample variation in high-quality contracts explained or fit by the independent variables.[17] Each alternative model is defined by adding the indicated variables to the first model in the group (the "standard models").

Table 2.7
Explanatory Power of Alternative Models of High-Quality Contract Production: Importance of Station- and Recruiter-Level Effects

Model	Proportion of Variance Explained
Individual production models:	
Standard model, excluding personal attributes	0.0324
Add personal attributes	0.0389
Station fixed effects	0.0744
Recruiter fixed effects	0.1776
Station production models:	
Standard model, excluding personal attributes	0.3275
Station fixed effects	0.4116
Recruiter fixed effects	0.4399

[16] This model links station-level enlistment outcomes with station-level missions and market characteristics and omits from the specification variables capturing the attributes or characteristics of individual recruiters within the station. However, the observational unit remains a recruiter-month, with the personal characteristics of recruiters pertaining to a single individual located in that station. Thus, a station with three recruiters has three different observations every month and, though the recruiter characteristics vary for each observation, the vector of station characteristics is identical. In future work it would be desirable to consider the mix of personnel and their characteristics located at a particular station.

[17] Table 2.7 reports results for regression analyses of both individual- and station-level data. Direct comparisons of explanatory power of different specifications are appropriate only across regression estimates for the same dependent variables. Thus, it is inappropriate to directly compare the fits of individual-level models with those of station-level models. See below for further discussion.

For the data on individual recruiters (top panel of Table 2.7), the explanatory power is rather low for all of the specifications. Adding variables on recruiter attributes increases the explanatory power very little (i.e., from 0.0324 to 0.0389). But the explanatory power more than doubles (from 0.0324) when station-level fixed effects (different regression intercepts for each station) are added. Table 2.7 also shows that the explanatory power of individual-level models increases considerably more from adding for fixed effects (different regression intercepts) for each recruiter than for each station.

A recruiter fixed effect represents the combined impacts of uncontrolled personal characteristics of that recruiter that are constant over months and make him or her more or less productive than other recruiters. These attributes can include the observable attributes used in the individual production models reported in Table 2.2 (which are excluded from the baseline or standard models in Table 2.7), as well as recruiter attributes for which we have no data, such as interpersonal skills, ambition, energy, training, and sales aptitude. In addition, these recruiter fixed effects could capture effects of market characteristics of the station's submarket for which the recruiter is responsible. Whatever the reason, these fixed effects increase the R-squared to 0.1776, more than 0.10 above the level explained when station-specific (rather than recruiter-specific) effects are included.

For the station-level data, the R-squared statistics are substantially higher, which reflects (to an unknown degree) the well-known tendency for aggregation of dependent variables to increase explanatory power.[18] In the case of station-level models, adding station fixed effects or recruiter fixed effects increases the R-squared statistics by roughly 25 and 34 percent, respectively. The higher explanatory power of the station-level model that includes recruiter fixed effects rather than station fixed effects strongly suggests important roles for unmeasured recruiter characteristics in determining productivity. Clearly, the observable attributes identified and included in the individual produc-

---

[18] Intuitively, such aggregation tends to average out random influences on the less-aggregated (here individual-level) dependent variable, thereby creating dependent variables that are less "noisy."

tion model (Table 2.2) play significant roles and can be influenced by a variety of recruiter-selection and assignment policies. However, the magnitude of systematic recruiter-level effects that are not captured by these included attributes suggests that much remains unknown about effects of recruiter attributes that we are unable to measure.

The existence of much higher R-squared statistics for the station-level models (compared with individual-level models) is partly a statistical artifact due to the tendency of random components of the individual-level production data to cancel out when they are aggregated over recruiters within each station.[19] But this increase in explanatory power is also likely to reflect (to an unknown degree) substantive reasons that station-level models could be preferable to individual-level models. One possibility is that the market variables used in estimating the models for both individual recruiters and stations relate to the stations' entire sales areas, but each recruiter in a multiple-recruiter station is usually responsible for a specific portion of the station's sales territory (e.g., high schools are generally assigned to specific recruiters). And, to the extent that the portions of a station's sales territory are heterogeneous, the market variables used in the regressions (which are constructed at the station level) are measured with error for individual recruiters.

Another reason that station-level models could be more informative is that the station is the relevant unit of performance, even though individual missions were assigned during this period. For example, station-level contracts appear to be more responsive than individual-level contracts to increases in missions. The station model coefficient of 0.2479 in Appendix A, Table A.4 suggests that a one-unit increase in mission allocated to a station (rather than an individual recruiter) can be expected, on average, to yield 0.2479 more high-quality contracts at the station level. This estimate is twice as large as the corresponding estimate of 0.1121 (Table 2.2), which pertains to the effect of a one-unit increase in a station's mission allocated to a particular recruiter. Since the typical station has between two and three recruiters, this

---

[19] Since this dataset oversamples stations with more recruiters, the average station size in the sample is 4.3 recruiters, even though stations had only 2.3 recruiters on average.

difference suggests that recruiters had team-oriented incentives and behavior even during our sample period, in which individual recruiters were assigned missions.

CHAPTER THREE

Mission Equity and Determinants of Achieving Station Missions

In this chapter we examine station-level missions and the factors that lead to success or failure in meeting them. The analysis focuses on station production of regular Army contracts from January 2001 through June 2003, when the Army used station missions.

Missioning is a key element of recruiter management. Most importantly, enlistment goals are the performance standards used to define success or failure in the recruiting business. Thus, how production targets are established and used to judge performance raises important equity and morale issues. A key motivation for our analysis is that many recruiters, as well as many in the Recruiting Command hierarchy, believe that many stations are assigned missions that are consistently too high or too low relative to the quality or potential of their local recruiting markets.

Furthermore, theoretical analysis suggests that missions, when effectively allocated, can induce extra recruiter effort and promote efficient use of recruiting resources. On the one hand, assigning missions that are exceptionally challenging can reduce morale and lead to lower effort. On the other hand, if missions are not challenging given market quality, recruiters may have little incentive to work hard to maximize production. During our period of analysis, the regular Army mission "box" consisted of three categories: (a) grad alphas, (b) senior alphas, and (c) all others.[1] This contrasts with earlier time periods during which

---

[1] For most of this period, graduate alphas could substitute for senior alphas and "others," and senior alphas could substitute for "others" (but not the reverse).

the mission box consisted of many more categories with separate targets for men and women as well as finer distinctions among AFQT
levels. In this chapter we focus on factors affecting the probability that
a station will achieve its regular Army mission.[2]

Before turning to our empirical analyses, it is useful to provide
some historical context. In early 2001, the Army was having trouble
meeting its rather ambitious high-quality contract mission, falling
short by an average of 40 percent up through the beginning of FY02.
As illustrated in Figure 3.1, in FY01 recruiting stations had an average
high-quality mission of 3.6 per month, but production averaged 2.5

Figure 3.1
High-Quality Contracts and Missions: Station Monthly Averages,
FY99–FY03

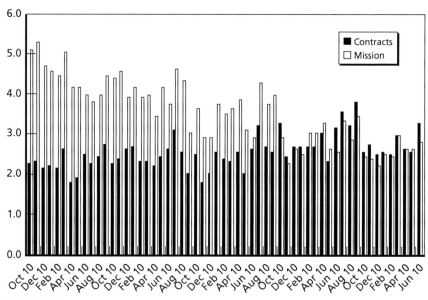

RAND MG433-3.1

---

[2]   More than half of the stations were also given Army reserve missions, and for those stations success requires meeting both the reserve and regular Army (RA) missions. However,
despite the evidence presented in Chapter Four that reserve and RA enlistments draw from
the same population, the competitive effects are small.

contracts. Such shortfalls were typical and more pronounced in FY99 and FY00, when missions were even more daunting.[3] Beginning in FY02, missions and contracts were more closely aligned, primarily due to the adoption of less ambitious goals.[4]

As a result, individual stations succeeded with greater frequency in FY02. As can be seen from Figure 3.2, in FY02 stations met monthly regular Army (RA) high-quality missions roughly 40 percent of the time as compared with just over 20 percent in FY01. The results for FY01 were themselves a significant improvement over the preceding years. For example, in the early part of FY99, success rates were much lower, at less than 10 percent. With the subsequent decreases in

Figure 3.2
Percentages of Stations Making Mission Box, FY99–FY03

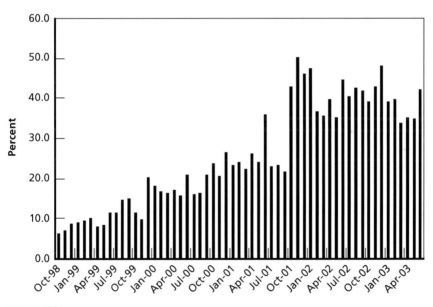

RAND MG433-3.2

---

[3] In particular, for FY99 and FY00 combined, stations had an average high-quality mission of 4.4 contracts and an average high-quality production of 2.5 contracts.

[4] For FY02, stations had an average high-quality mission of 2.9 contracts and an average high-quality production of 3.0 contracts.

missions, stations were more successful.   During the sample period from January 2001 through June 2003, stations made their regular Army missions about 36 percent of the time.[5]

The Station Production Data

The station-level data analyzed in this chapter and Chapters Four and Five are described in Table 3.1. Information describing recruiting stations, their staffing and production levels, and local markets was gathered for the more than 1,600 stations for the 30-month period. The dataset contained over 42,000 observations (station-month pairs). Table 3.1 provides variable definitions as well as the sample means and standard deviations for these variables, grouped by category.[6]

Our dependent variables focus on two outcomes, namely, the number of high-quality contracts and the probability of making *regular Army* mission box. The average number of high-quality contracts (gross of DEP losses) was just under three per station per month. The typical station made regular Army mission box about 36 percent of the time.

Mission variables included the two high-quality categories (test categories I-IIIA seniors and graduates), as well as other regular Army missions. Data on losses from the Delayed Entry Program (DEP) were also gathered. To succeed in a given month, the station must write a contract for each mission plus any DEP losses charged that month, category by category (in some cases, after applying substitution rules). Thus, a DEP loss is equivalent to an increase in the mission for that recruit category.

The number of "on-production" regular Army recruiters (OPRA) in a station averaged about 2.3 over the sample period. About 27 percent of the stations had but a single recruiter, and almost 15 percent had four or more production recruiters.

---

[5]   During this same period, USAREC achieved its (national-level) high-quality contracts mission only once; specifically, in March 2003.

[6]   More detailed information about these data is presented in Appendix C.

Although our focus was on regular Army recruiting, information was also collected on U.S. Army reserve (USAR) recruiters, missions, and DEP losses. About 57 percent of stations are assigned separate reserve missions and recruiters. In total, the reserve recruiter force was just over 20 percent of the RA recruiting manpower over this time period. Although USAR missions are set independently of those for the regular Army, there are several reasons that they should be included as explanatory variables in the models described below. First, it is likely that reserve and RA recruiting draw from the same high school senior and graduate pools. Thus, regular Army and USAR recruiters compete and could negatively affect each other. On the other hand, there could be positive spillovers if recruiters truly behave as members of the same team. As explained above, to be successful, a station with a USAR mission must achieve both its reserve and regular Army missions. To the

Table 3.1
Monthly Station-Level Data, January 2001 to June 2003

Variable		Description	Mean	Standard Deviation
Dependent variables:				
Y	Contracts	Number of gross high-quality contracts (AFQT I–IIIA graduates and seniors)	2.9488	2.1452
P	Box	Made regular Army mission box (0,1)	0.3568	0.4791
Regular Army (RA) mission variables:				
Q_t	Mission plus DEP loss	High-quality mission (AFQT I–IIIA graduates and seniors) plus DEP losses	3.6445	1.9746
Q_m	Mission	High-quality mission (AFQT I–IIIA graduates and seniors)	3.2046	1.6526
Q_d	DEP loss	High-quality DEP losses (AFQT I–IIIA graduates and seniors)	0.4399	.3444
S_m	Senior	High-quality senior mission per recruiter	0.4527	0.3924
G_m	Graduate	High-quality graduate mission per recruiter	1.1184	0.7663
S_d	Senior DEP	Senior DEP attrition per recruiter	0.0867	0.2753
G_d	Graduate DEP	Graduate DEP attrition per recruiter	0.1210	0.2876

Table 3.1—continued

Variable		Description	Mean	Standard Deviation
R	Ratio	Ratio of production to mission for previous year, lagged 3 months, high-quality only	0.8147	0.2869
Recruiter variables:				
Rec	Recruiters	On-production, regular Army recruiters (OPRA)	2.3285	1.1164
x_1	2-recruiter station	Dichotomous variable = 1 when there are 2 recruiters on production	0.3584	0.4795
x_2	3-recruiter station	Dichotomous variable = 1 when there are 3 recruiters on production	0.2350	0.4240
x_3	4-recruiter station	Dichotomous variable = 1 when there are 4 recruiters on production	0.1084	0.3109
x_4	5-recruiter station	Dichotomous variable = 1 when there are 5 recruiters on production	0.0344	0.1823
x_5	6+ recruiter station	Dichotomous variable = 1 when there are 6 or more recruiters on production	0.0075	0.0862
Reserve variables:				
x_6	Reserve recruiters	Reserve recruiters divided by number of OPRA recruiters	0.2303	0.3438
x_7	Reserve mission, "other"	Reserve mission, "other," divided by number of OPRA recruiters	0.1822	0.3165
x_8	Reserve mission, prior service	Reserve mission, prior service, divided by number of OPRA recruiters	0.2531	0.4855
x_9	Reserve mission, high school	Reserve mission, high school, divided by number of OPRA recruiters	0.0936	0.1065
x_{10}	DEP loss, "other" reserves	DEP loss, "other" reserves, divided by number of OPRA recruiters	0.0465	0.1868
x_{11}	DEP loss, prior service reserves	DEP loss, prior service reserves, divided by number of OPRA recruiters	0.0012	0.0277
x_{12}	DEP loss, high school reserves	DEP loss, high school reserves, divided by number of OPRA recruiters	0.0812	0.2548
Other mission variable:				
x_{13}	Mission, "other" Regular Army	Number of "other" mission per OPRA recruiters	0.9859	0.7013

Table 3.1—continued

Variable	Description	Mean	Standard Deviation
Month indicator variables:			
x_{14} February	Dichotomous variable = 1 for the month of February	0.1019	0.3025
x_{15} March	Dichotomous variable = 1 for the month of March	0.1028	0.3036
x_{16} April	Dichotomous variable = 1 for the month of April	0.1029	0.3038
x_{17} May	Dichotomous variable = 1 for the month of May	0.1027	0.3035
x_{18} June	Dichotomous variable = 1 for the month of June	0.0699	0.2550
x_{19} July	Dichotomous variable = 1 for the month of July	0.0706	0.2562
x_{20} August	Dichotomous variable = 1 for the month of August	0.0702	0.2554
x_{21} September	Dichotomous variable = 1 for the month of September	0.0704	0.2559
x_{22} October	Dichotomous variable = 1 for the month of October	0.0707	0.2563
x_{23} November	Dichotomous variable = 1 for the month of November	0.0697	0.2546
x_{24} December	Dichotomous variable = 1 for the month of December	0.0685	0.2526
Region indicator variables:			
x_{25} Mountain	Dichotomous variable = 1 for stations located in Mountain states	0.0768	0.2663
x_{26} North Central	Dichotomous variable = 1 for stations located in North Central states	0.2440	0.4295
x_{27} South	Dichotomous variable = 1 for stations located in Southern states	0.3749	0.4841
x_{28} Pacific	Dichotomous variable = 1 for stations located in Pacific Coast states	0.1331	0.3397
Local climate variables:			
x_{29} Hot	Average July temperature (.1 degrees)	753.4760	79.5839
x_{30} Rain	July precipitation (.01 inches)	345.5731	204.9836

Table 3.1—continued

Variable		Description	Mean	Standard Deviation
x_{31}	Humidity	July humidity (percent)	57.7458	15.1000
Personnel status variables:				
x_{32}	Commanders, on production	On-production commanders, divided by total number of on-production recruiters	0.2059	0.3291
x_{33}	Recruiters on duty	Recruiters on duty, not assigned to production, divided by total on-production recruiters	0.1152	0.2649
x_{34}	Absent recruiters	Recruiters not on production, absent, divided by total on-production recruiters	0.1362	0.3845
x_{35}	Commanders, not on production	Commanders not on production, divided by total number of on-production recruiters	0.1258	0.2673
Market variables:				
x_{36}	QMA per recruiter	Qualified military available population, per OPRA, in logarithms	6.4611	0.6723
x_{37}	Unemployment change	Change in unemployment rate since last month, in logarithms	0.0146	0.1112
x_{38}	Unemployment level	Unemployment rate, in logarithms	1.6258	0.3584
x_{39}	Relative wage	Manufacturing earnings, divided by E-4 monthly compensation, in logarithms	−4.6476	0.1291
Demographic variables:				
x_{40}	Black	Ratio of black to total males	0.1280	0.1417
x_{41}	Hispanic	Ratio of Hispanic to total males	0.1365	0.1957
x_{42}	College	Percentage of male population in college	43.2813	4.5303
x_{43}	Urban population	Ratio of urban to total population	0.5348	0.3838
x_{44}	Clustered population	Ratio of clustered to total population	0.1675	0.1836
x_{45}	Growth in single parent homes	Ratio of single-parent households in 2000 to single-parent households in 1990	1.3747	0.2577
x_{46}	Poverty	Ratio of children in poverty to total population	0.0069	0.0043
x_{47}	Catholic	Ratio of Catholics in total population	0.1904	0.1425

Table 3.1—continued

Variable		Description	Mean	Standard Deviation
x_{48}	Eastern religion	Ratio of Eastern religion adherents in total population	0.0037	0.0068
x_{49}	Christian	Ratio of non-Catholic Christian adherents in total population	0.0870	0.0651
Veteran population variables:				
x_{50}	Vet pop < 32	Ratio of veteran population aged 32 or under to male population (17–21)	0.1735	0.0462
x_{51}	Vet pop 33–42	Ratio of veteran population between 33 and 42 to male population (17–21)	0.3225	0.1018
x_{52}	Vet pop 43–55	Ratio of veteran population between 43 and 55 to male population (17–21)	0.7277	0.2079
x_{53}	Vet pop 56–65	Ratio of veteran population between 56 and 65 to male population (17–21)	0.5569	0.1640
x_{54}	Vet pop 65–72	Ratio of veteran population between 65 and 72 to male population (17–21)	0.3997	0.1202
x_{55}	Vet pop 73+	Ratio of veteran population 73 or older to male population (17–21)	0.6178	0.2496
Competition variable:				
x_{56}	Army market share	Army contracts as a percentage of total DoD enlistment contracts, 1999	34.5661	7.8885

extent that making mission overall is a valued performance goal, the existence of a reserve mission would alter the probability of being successful and, therefore, affect regular Army recruiter incentives as well.

Several dichotomous (0,1) indicator variables representing seasonal and regional fixed effects were included. These include a variable representing each calendar month and one for each of five regions, the Northeast, Mountain, North Central, South, and Pacific.

Information was also gathered on local climate, specifically, July average temperature, total precipitation, and humidity index. For the sample, the July temperatures averaged 75 degrees and rainfall averaged 3.5 inches. The humidity index, which reflects the number of hours of "high humidity" in July, averaged over 57 with a standard deviation of 15.

Additional information on the staffing at each station was also collected, with all of these variables expressed per OPRA. These included the number of assigned recruiters on duty, but not on full production; the number of recruiters assigned, but temporarily on leave; and station commanders with limited or no responsibility to sign prospects.

Several market and demographic variables were collected. These included the qualified military available population (QMA) per OPRA recruiter, expressed in natural logarithms. On average, per-recruiter QMA was about 650 youth. Also included were local economic factors, including the relative civilian to military wage rate and unemployment conditions (expressed as the logarithms of the unemployment rate and its month-to-month change). Demographic variables included population proportions of blacks, Hispanics, males enrolled in college, residents of urban areas, and residents of population "clusters."[7] Also included were a measure of childhood poverty and a measure of growth in single-parent households. Finally, we also included measures of local populations reporting affiliation with a variety of organized religions, including Catholicism, Eastern religions (such as Buddhism and Hinduism), and Christian adherents other than Catholics.

Several variables representing prevalence of (all services') veterans in 2001 were also included to capture effects of veterans as influencers, role models, or local attitudes toward military service. Because these influences may be quite different depending on the era of service (World War II versus Vietnam versus Persian Gulf, for example), these measures were broken up into six subgroups based on age.

Our final measure was included to represent the strength of competition from the other services. Because the current share of the Army in a given market (Army enlistments as a percentage of enlistments into all four services) is likely to be endogenous, the share as of 1999

---

[7] The U.S. Census Bureau defines urban, rural, and clustered populations as follows: "urban areas . . . include urbanized areas and urban clusters. An urban area generally consists of a large central place and adjacent densely settled census blocks that together have a total population of at least 2,500 for urban clusters, or at least 50,000 for urbanized areas. . . Rural . . . population [is population] not classified as urban." http://askcensus.gov, accessed on May 12, 2005.

was included.[8] The Army share averaged almost 35 percent of all enlistments with a standard deviation of almost 8, and the Army market share was between 27 and 43 for about 95 percent of the stations.

Logistic Regressions of Making Regular Army Missions

In this section we provide estimates of descriptive models of station performance and simulate the effects of changes in key factors. The logistic regressions provide quantitative estimates of the roles of a variety of factors on the probability that an individual station will fail to achieve its regular Army mission box, taking into account the substitution rules prevailing at the time. The first set of estimates, reported in Table 3.2, examines all 56 of the explanatory variables described above as well as controls for senior and graduate I-IIIA mission levels and DEP losses. Not surprisingly, increases in the performance goals lead to significant declines in the probability of succeeding. DEP losses are even more conducive to failure than mission increases because their timing may come as a surprise, and they are added to already challenging targets, thereby making success even more unlikely.

Regular Army high-quality mission variables are included in the regressions reported in Table 3.2. As a result, coefficient estimates for other variables determine (through the logistic distribution function) the marginal effects of these variables on the probability of not making mission—or the difficulty of making mission—controlling for any adjustments in mission allocations that may have been made to equalize difficulty. For example, station size appears to matter, with one-recruiter stations (the omitted category) having a considerably higher probability of making mission, and a tendency for the probability of making mission to decline for increasingly large station sizes given any adjustments of missions associated with station size.

---

[8] As reported in Chapter Two, Army share data were not available for about 10 percent of the station areas, and the missing data were replaced by predicted values derived from a regression equation reported in Appendix A, Table A.1.

Table 3.2
Logistic Regression Results: Probability of Failing to Make Regular Army Mission, Holding Mission Constant

	Variable	Coefficient	Standard Error
Intercept		1.8774	0.5986
S_m	High-quality senior mission per recruiter	0.6111	0.0330
G_m	High-quality graduate mission per recruiter	0.9175	0.0246
S_d	Senior DEP attrition per recruiter	1.0572	0.0567
G_d	Graduate DEP attrition per recruiter	1.0490	0.0468
x_1	2-recruiter station	0.3942	0.0341
x_2	3-recruiter station	0.4563	0.0428
x_3	4-recruiter station	0.5016	0.0529
x_4	5-recruiter station	0.4796	0.0718
x_5	6+ recruiter station	0.5771	0.1263
x_6	Reserve recruiters per OPRA	−0.4689	0.0428
x_7	Reserve mission, "other" per OPRA	0.0058	0.0412
x_8	Reserve mission, prior service per OPRA	0.2085	0.0303
x_9	Reserve mission, high school per OPRA	0.7732	0.1318
x_{10}	DEP loss, "other" reserves per OPRA	0.0754	0.0623
x_{11}	DEP loss, prior service reserves per OPRA	0.3086	0.4142
x_{12}	DEP loss, high school reserves per OPRA	−0.2085	0.0461
x_{13}	Mission, "other" regular Army per OPRA	0.1974	0.0211
x_{14}	February	0.0684	0.0519
x_{15}	March	0.1607	0.0526
x_{16}	April	−0.0142	0.0531
x_{17}	May	0.3076	0.0520
x_{18}	June	−0.2541	0.0544
x_{19}	July	−0.2546	0.0589
x_{20}	August	−0.1433	0.0595
x_{21}	September	−0.0877	0.0582
x_{22}	October	−0.1407	0.0520
x_{23}	November	−0.0023	0.0499
x_{24}	December	−0.1090	0.0513
x_{25}	Mountain	−0.0072	0.0656

Table 3.2—continued

	Variable	Coefficient	Standard Error
x_{26}	North Central	−0.1689	0.0414
x_{27}	South	−0.3666	0.0509
x_{28}	Pacific	−0.0849	0.0612
x_{29}	Hot	−0.0007	0.0002
x_{30}	Rain	−0.0001	0.0001
x_{31}	Humidity	0.0053	0.0012
x_{32}	Commanders, on production	0.2230	0.0410
x_{33}	Recruiters on duty	−0.9652	0.0822
x_{34}	Absent recruiters	−0.6271	0.0358
x_{35}	Commanders, not on production	0.2073	0.0817
x_{36}	QMA per recruiter	−0.1407	0.0249
x_{37}	Unemployment change	−0.4118	0.1098
x_{38}	Unemployment level	−0.3110	0.0362
x_{39}	Relative wage	0.2165	0.1139
x_{40}	Black	0.9235	0.1318
x_{41}	Hispanic	0.3644	0.1023
x_{42}	College	−0.0015	0.0028
x_{43}	Urban population	−0.0616	0.0832
x_{44}	Cluster population	0.1145	0.1299
x_{45}	Growth in single parent homes	−0.0218	0.0047
x_{46}	Poverty	30.1755	3.8278
x_{47}	Catholic	0.3299	0.1307
x_{48}	Eastern Religion	−1.1739	2.1117
x_{49}	Christian	−0.2706	0.2013
x_{50}	Vet pop < 32	0.0815	0.5208
x_{51}	Vet pop 33–42	−2.6047	0.3800
x_{52}	Vet pop 43–55	1.1756	0.1918
x_{53}	Vet pop 56–65	−0.9091	0.2104
x_{54}	Vet pop 65–72	1.6334	0.3382
x_{55}	Vet pop 73+	−0.2607	0.1075
x_{56}	Army market share	−0.0069	0.0015

The negative estimated coefficient for reserve recruiters per OPRA (x_6) suggests that the presence of reserve recruiters confers positive spillovers on RA recruiting, other things equal; but the positive coefficients on the prior service and high school reserve mission variables (x_8 and x_9) indicate that this beneficial effect is eliminated if the USAR recruiters are given sufficiently large missions. This may be due to a tendency for large reserve missions to lead to higher reserve enlistments and thereby deplete the pool of candidates available to sign RA contracts. Not surprisingly, the impact of increasing a USAR mission on regular Army recruiting is greater for candidates currently in high school than for those with prior military service. Interestingly, a high school reserve DEP loss has a positive impact on regular Army recruiting, most likely because reserve DEP losses often occur when a committed future reservist decides to enlist in the regular Army instead.

Many of the monthly and regional variables have significant and substantial effects. Convincing a prospect to sign a contract in May is particularly difficult and much easier in June through August. Relative to the Northeast (the excluded regional category), making a given mission is easier in all other regions, especially in the South (although the estimate for the Pacific region is not statistically significant). We interpret these results as describing patterns that are beyond the control of USAREC or recruiters.

Staffing differences can also be quite important. For example, temporary duties or absences of RA recruiters are associated with higher probabilities of RA success for the station. One interpretation is that the flow of contracts in a month with recruiters not on production may be higher because of past efforts of the recruiters who are not on production. Another plausible interpretation is that a market that is promising enough to support multiple recruiters (and, hence, is more likely to have assigned recruiters who are not on production) offers an abundance of prospects for the recruiters who are on production.

The market variables and most of the demographic variables had significant effects in the expected directions. Mission success is less likely when local civilian wages are higher and more likely when unemployment rates are high, increasing, or both. The larger the population of qualified prospects per recruiter, the easier it is to make mission.

Missions are more difficult to achieve in areas with high percentages of minority populations and when poverty rates are high. Prevalence of certain religious groups appears to matter. In particular, Catholics are slightly less likely to enlist. The effects of veteran populations depend on the veteran-age cohort. For example, a higher prevalence of veterans aged 33 to 42 has a positive impact on mission accomplishment, while a greater presence of veterans aged 43 to 55 has the opposite effect.

Simulated effects of changes in selected key factors are presented in Table 3.3. Scenarios are defined relative to a baseline representing the average market in which the probability of making mission box is about 33 percent. If one adds a senior alpha mission to a station's mission, the probability of success falls to 20.1 percent, a decline of 12.9 percentage points. Adding a grad alpha to the mission has an even bigger impact, with a predicted decline to 17.0 percent. In contrast, an additional mission for the "other" category has about one-third of the impact on mission difficulty.

This ratio of about three to one in the difficulty of obtaining high-quality versus other contracts is similar to estimates obtained from past efforts to estimate the tradeoff directly, using a production possibility

Table 3.3
Simulations from Logistic Model Holding Missions Constant

Simulated Scenario	Probability of RA Boxing (%)
Baseline (sample average)	33.0
Add grad alpha mission	17.0
Add senior alpha mission	20.1
6 or more recruiters	28.4
No reserve recruiting	33.0
Add "other mission"	28.1
Unemployment falls by 50%	28.8
May	26.3
June	38.3

approach.[9] This result suggests that the current recruiter incentive system, which provides relative points for high- versus lower-quality categories at a 2:1 ratio, may underreward high quality.[10]

In comparing stations with a reserve mission to those without one, the simulations indicate that the total impact is essentially zero. That is, the probability of making a given regular Army mission is the same when one takes into account both economies of joint production (positive spillovers) and negative effects of depleting the pool of candidates.

Interestingly, a 50 percent reduction in the unemployment rate would lower the probability of success to 28.8 percent. While significant, this probability is similar to that for recruiting stations with six or more recruiters or for the average station during the month of May. This result suggests that seasonal mission adjustments or accurate accounting for differences between stations based on size may be as important as the economy.

We now turn to simulations performed to gauge the importance for explaining sample variation in high-quality contracts of subsets of variables included in the logistic regression reported in Table 3.2. For these simulations, the predicted contributions for subsets of variables were computed for each observation in the sample, and the measure of importance is the sample standard deviation of these contributions.[11] So the computed measures of importance reflect estimated logistic regression coefficients as well as the amounts of sample variation and covariation of selected independent variables. Table 3.4 reports the results.

---

[9]   Dertouzos (1985) and Polich, Dertouzos, and Press (1986) estimate the average tradeoff between high and lower quality enlistments to be between 3 and 4.

[10]   In addition, implementation of team production provides individual mission box achievement points when the station makes mission and the individual recruiter signs at least one contract of any category.

[11]   The method for computing these measures of importance of groups of variables is analogous to that used to calculate the measures in Table 2.6, but in the present case it involves an additional step of converting the sums of variables times their coefficients to predicted probabilities using the logistic distribution function. These measures account for correlations between variables within subsets and provide a relative measure of the importance of a subset of variables in generating sample-wide variability in the probability of making RA mission.

Table 3.4
Importance of Subsets of Variables Included in the Logistic Regression for Predicting Regular Army Mission Success

	One standard deviation below mean	One standard deviation above mean	Range
Model predictions	0.165	0.572	0.406
RA mission—missions	0.183	0.542	0.359
RA mission—DEP losses	0.244	0.450	0.206
Personnel status	0.261	0.428	0.166
Demographics	0.283	0.401	0.119
Recruiter—station size	0.297	0.386	0.089
Reserve	0.298	0.384	0.087
Market	0.303	0.379	0.076
Competition	0.320	0.359	0.039

NOTES: (1) Subsets of variables described in the first column are named according to the groups of variables with corresponding names listed in Table 3.1 of which they are subsets. But these subsets include only those variables included in the logistic regression reported in Table 3.2. (2) Cell entries are predicted probabilities of making regular Army mission.

The complete model provides predictions with mean minus one standard deviation of 0.165 and mean plus one standard deviation of 0.572. The range between these values is used as a benchmark to gauge the importance of the subsets of variables reported in the table, with these subsets ordered by decreasing importance.

Perhaps not surprisingly, the most important subsets of variables for predicting the probability of making RA mission are the mission and DEP loss variables that are used by the Army as the standard for success. In particular, variation in RA mission levels per recruiter is the most important factor that affects monthly success, with a prediction range of 0.359. The RA DEP loss variables are also quite important, with a range of 0.206. Note that these results reflect more than mere arithmetic; they also reflect behavioral responses of recruiters to changes in goals. More specifically—as we emphasize and examine empirically in Chapter Four—when missions or DEP losses are higher, recruiters will tend to work harder, and (as a result) enlistments will tend to increase to some extent. The results reported in Chapter Four indicate, however, that a one-unit increase in missions or DEP losses increases enlistments by less than one unit on average. Hence increases in missions or DEP losses tend to decrease the average probability of making mission, as reflected in results reported in Table 3.4.

Next in importance is staffing, at 16.6 percentage points. Demographics, production recruiters, and reserve recruiting variables follow. It is important to note that even though reserve recruiting has no effect on RA outcomes on average, variations in reserve variables significantly affect outcomes from one station-month to another. Reserve factors, surprisingly, are even more important than market factors.

Equity of Missions

The analysis reported in the previous section controlled for missions. For that reason, the estimated coefficients for other variables can be interpreted as representing the incremental impact of a variety of factors on mission difficulty, holding mission levels constant. However, missions are presumably allocated, at least partially, with equity considerations in mind.[12] To equalize difficulty, the *ex ante* probability of making mission, given equal levels of effort and talent, would need to be the same across all markets. In other words, missions would be allocated to account for differences in market quality across the territories of different stations.

To examine the extent to which the difficulty of making RA mission varies and the predictors of these differences, an additional logistic regression analysis was conducted, using the same data and a nearly identical model. The key difference was the exclusion of the high-quality RA mission variables. The interpretations of the resulting coefficient estimates, which are reported in Table 3.5, are the marginal impacts of station-specific, market, and demographic factors on the probability

---

[12] Of course, missions are also set with production (efficiency) goals in mind. In Chapter Four we derive a condition under which a mission allocation can both (a) equalize the difficulty of making mission across stations (and, thereby, satisfy an appealing definition of equity), and (b) maximize expected production at the national level. Empirical results reported in Chapter Four, however, indicate that this condition is not satisfied, and we conclude that there is generally a conflict between equity and efficiency in allocating missions.

Table 3.5
Logistic Regression Results: Probability of Failing to Make Regular Army High-Quality Missions, Not Controlling for These Missions

	Variable	Coefficient	Standard Error
	Intercept	0.5344	0.5803
x_1	2-recruiter station	0.0105	0.0318
x_2	3-recruiter station	−0.0960	0.0398
x_3	4-recruiter station	−0.1582	0.0496
x_4	5-recruiter station	−0.2447	0.0687
x_5	6+ recruiter station	−0.2172	0.1238
x_6	Reserve recruiters	−0.3879	0.0400
x_7	Reserve mission, "other"	0.0165	0.0388
x_8	Reserve mission, prior service	0.2845	0.0285
x_9	Reserve mission, high school	0.7101	0.1274
x_{10}	DEP loss, "other" reserves	0.0660	0.0583
x_{11}	DEP loss, prior service reserves	0.3792	0.3967
x_{12}	DEP loss, high school reserves	−0.1683	0.0431
x_{13}	Mission, "other" regular Army	0.4418	0.0193
x_{14}	February	0.1132	0.0501
x_{15}	March	0.2340	0.0509
x_{16}	April	0.0965	0.0513
x_{17}	May	0.2969	0.0503
x_{18}	June	−0.1541	0.0516
x_{19}	July	0.1372	0.0555
x_{20}	August	0.0858	0.0567
x_{21}	September	0.2326	0.0556
x_{22}	October	−0.0327	0.0497
x_{23}	November	−0.1287	0.0481
x_{24}	December	−0.2404	0.0495
x_{25}	Mountain	−0.0711	0.0636
x_{26}	North Central	−0.2356	0.0402
x_{27}	South	−0.3018	0.0492
x_{28}	Pacific	0.0552	0.0590
x_{29}	Hot	−0.0004	0.0002
x_{30}	Rain	0.0002	0.0001

Table 3.5—continued

	Variable	Coefficient	Standard Error
x_{31}	Humidity	0.0015	0.0012
x_{32}	Commanders, on production	−0.0349	0.0391
x_{33}	Recruiters on duty	−0.3757	0.0767
x_{34}	Absent recruiters	−0.3859	0.0327
x_{35}	Commanders, not on production	0.2824	0.0771
x_{36}	QMA per recruiter	0.1003	0.0237
x_{37}	Unemployment change	−0.2930	0.1060
x_{38}	Unemployment level	0.4299	0.0349
x_{39}	Relative wage	0.0548	0.1104
x_{40}	Black	1.0033	0.1275
x_{41}	Hispanic	0.5876	0.0996
x_{42}	College	−0.0032	0.0027
x_{43}	Urban population	0.0903	0.0807
x_{44}	Cluster population	0.1305	0.1261
x_{45}	Growth in single parent homes	−0.0084	0.0044
x_{46}	Poverty	32.3342	3.7444
x_{47}	Catholic	0.2241	0.1266
x_{48}	Eastern religion	−0.6268	2.0210
x_{49}	Christian	−0.4835	0.1940
x_{50}	Vet pop < 32	0.6820	0.5036
x_{51}	Vet pop 33–42	−2.2999	0.3652
x_{52}	Vet pop 43–55	1.5141	0.1843
x_{53}	Vet pop 56–65	−1.8644	0.2027
x_{54}	Vet pop 65–72	2.4071	0.3260
x_{55}	Vet pop 73+	−0.4136	0.1036
x_{56}	Market share	−0.0030	0.0014

of making RA mission, *allowing the mission to vary* with these factors according to historical patterns. If missions were accurately adjusted to offset variations in local conditions, then these coefficient estimates would be expected to be close to zero. Intuitively, if missions were allocated to give all stations the same probability of succeeding in making their RA missions—an appealing standard for equity—then the probability of success should not depend to any important degree on variables reflecting station-specific, market, or demographic factors.[13]

It appears that this is far from the case. For example, larger recruiting stations are more likely to succeed than are one-recruiter stations. Recall that the previous model estimates (Table 3.2), holding mission constant, indicated the opposite, namely that larger stations have lower probabilities of succeeding. In combination, then, these results indicate that the mission allocation process is overcompensating larger stations by allocating a lower-than-equitable share of mission. Table 3.6 summarizes the importance of subsets of variables implied by the results reported in Table 3.5. The methods used and results reported in the table are analogous to those in Table 3.4.

Table 3.6
Importance of Groups of Variables for Regular Army Mission Success, Not Holding High-Quality Regular Army Missions Constant

	One standard deviation below mean	One standard deviation above mean	Range
Model predictions	0.239	0.474	0.235
Demographics	0.295	0.402	0.107
Monthly effects	0.309	0.387	0.078
Reserve presence	0.312	0.383	0.071
Market	0.312	0.383	0.071
Personnel status	0.315	0.380	0.065
Regional effects	0.319	0.376	0.056
Recruiter—station size	0.330	0.364	0.034
Competition	0.341	0.353	0.012

NOTES: (1) Subsets of variables described in the first column are named according to the groups of variables with corresponding names listed in Table 3.1 of which they are subsets. But these subsets include only those variables included in the logistic regression reported in Table 3.5. (2) Cell entries are predicted probabilities of making regular Army mission.

---

[13] As emphasized and analyzed in Chapter Four, the effects of higher or lower missions on expected contract levels (and, hence, the probability of making mission) are moderated by recruiter responses in terms of effort expended. But these effort responses do not change expected contracts by as much as missions change.

In this model, in which high-quality RA missions are allowed to vary, predicted probabilities range from 23.9 percent to 47.4 percent, compared with a 16.5 percent to 57.2 percent range for the model that holds these missions constant (Table 3.4). Clearly, the mission-setting process equalizes mission difficulty somewhat, but falls significantly short of complete equalization. The most important categories in accounting for variations in difficulty, listed in descending order of importance, are demographic factors, monthly effects,[14] reserve presence, market factors, and staffing.

Table 3.7 lists the ten most important characteristics of stations that should be given lower relative missions, other things equal, if fairness is the goal.[15] This ranking was determined by comparing the impacts of one-standard-deviation increases in the variables from their means on the predicted probability of making mission. For example, a one-standard-deviation increase in the "other" regular Army mission variable from its mean (an increase from 0.98 to 1.69) would lower the probability of success by a bit over 14 percent. This implies that other missions are not being properly considered, if fairness is the objective, in setting targets for high-quality categories. Other variables include veteran populations between 43 and 55 years old and between 65 and 72. Even with adjustments of missions, station markets with large proportions of blacks or Hispanics and high poverty rates have lower probabilities of success. Finally, if equity is the goal, missions in May and March should be adjusted downward, as should RA missions in markets with high reserve missions for candidates with prior military service and high school students.

In Table 3.8, results of an analogous analysis are presented, but this time for the top ten candidates for increasing relative missions,

---

[14] If a recruiter is in a market in which it is typically easy to make mission, month-to-month variation in difficulty of making mission may not raise substantial equity concerns. For other recruiters, however, failure or inability (because missions must take on integer values) to smooth missions over time may be very important from an equity point of view.

[15] Note that the results under discussion pertain to the equity benefits of changing missions in particular ways and do not address the costs of doing so. Such costs, of course, are highly relevant to policy choices.

Table 3.7
Top Ten Candidates for Decreasing Missions to Promote Equity

Variable	Impact on Prob of RA Success
Mission, "other" RA	−0.1408
Vet pop 43–55	−0.1222
Vet pop 65–72	−0.0858
Hispanic	−0.0647
Reserve mission, prior service	−0.0571
Black	−0.0551
Poverty	−0.0529
May	−0.0424
March	−0.0332
Reserve mission, high school	−0.0330

Table 3.8
Top Ten Candidates for Increasing Missions to Promote Equity

Variable	Impact on Prob of RA Success
Vet pop 33–42	0.1031
Vet pop 56–65	0.0875
Absent recruiter	0.0618
Reserve recruiters	0.0589
South	0.0586
Unemployment level	0.0581
Christian	0.0476
Recruiter on duty	0.0423
December	0.0418
North Central	0.0378

other things equal. During the sample period, missions were under-allocated to markets with large values of the listed variables. Again, veteran populations are not adequately considered. Currently, mission success is more probable in markets with relatively high proportions of veterans between the ages of 33 and 42 and 56 and 65. Stations are more likely to succeed in markets when assigned recruiters are absent, suggesting that stations with temporarily reduced manpower are given lower-than-equitable missions. To promote equity, missions might also be increased in relative terms for stations in the South and North Central regions, in areas with high unemployment rates, and during December.

Reserve Missions and Equity

The previous results indicate that the probability of making the RA mission box is largely unaffected by the presence of reserve recruiting. However, Table 3.9 shows that only about 40 percent of the stations having an USAR mission actually make that mission. Thus, the joint probability of making both sets of missions—which is required for station success and station bonus points—is much lower, at 16.7 percent. The upshot is that stations with USAR missions (in addition to RA missions) have much lower probabilities of success.[16]

Performance Evaluation and Mission Success

If the goal of missioning is equity, the current process fails to account adequately for systematic differences between stations in their likelihood of being successful. These differences stem from factors such as prevailing local market conditions, staff composition, station size, and seasonal and regional differences. As a result, much of the distinction

---

[16] In the analysis of station production of high-quality RA contracts reported in Chapter Four, there is no evidence that, *on average*, the presence of reserve recruiters and missions significantly affects production of high-quality, regular Army contracts. Thus, the lower probability of overall mission box success for stations with USAR missions does not appear to have much of an impact one way or another. Further analysis is desirable to probe this rather striking result. However, there is considerable variation from station to station, depending on the size of the reserve mission relative to the number of reserve recruiters. Thus, there are productivity gains that are possible if the allocation of RA missions were adjusted to reflect this variation.

Table 3.9
Relationship Between Mission Box Success and Reserve Recruiting

	Station Category:	
	Station has Regular Army mission only	Station has RA plus USAR mission
Percent of sample stations	42.6%	57.4%
Made RA mission box	37.2%	34.6%
Made USAR mission box	NA*	39.9%
Made overall mission box	37.2%	16.7%

*Not applicable, since these stations have RA mission only.

between successful and unsuccessful stations is attributable to factors having nothing to do with the effort, ability, and leadership of recruiting personnel.

Moreover, the analysis of individual recruiter performance in Chapter Two indicates that some recruiters are consistently more productive than others, but that only a small part of these differences can be predicted or explained by observable recruiter characteristics such as age, education, race, gender, occupational specialty, and assignment. As a result, the Army is faced with a management challenge of identifying and then rewarding successful recruiters and recruiting stations, while accounting for systematic differences in the difficulty of missions. To achieve this, the Army could develop and use a more effective model for assigning missions *ex ante* (one such model is presented in Chapter Four) or, alternatively, evaluate performance *ex post* and explicitly compare performance with a metric that accounts for differences in mission difficulty.

One such method for identifying differences in performance might simply be to examine levels of success over a period or window longer than a single month.[17] For example, for six-month windows during the period from January 2001 through June 2003, 16 percent

---

[17] Longer performance windows might also enable the Army to move toward a system of allowing stations to "bank" contracts that exceed their current monthly missions (i.e., overproduction relative to mission) so they can be used to make up shortfalls (i.e., underproduction relative to mission) in subsequent months within the performance window. An advantage of this approach would be that it provides stronger incentives for overproduction.

of stations failed to achieve the regular Army mission box even once. Table 3.10 provides the distribution of success rates. Another 25 percent of the stations made mission a single time. In contrast, a few stations were highly successful, with 2 percent making their missions all six months and about 5 percent meeting performance goals in five out of six months.

Since effective human resource management requires identifying and rewarding good performers and replacing bad ones, an obvious question emerges: To what extent do differences in medium-term success rates distinguish good and bad performers? For example, are those recruiters failing for six consecutive months truly worse than those who have made mission box several times during that same period? Our analyses of mission box success hint at the answer. In particular, since much of the monthly differences are due either to imperfect missioning or randomness, many of the low achievers may be victims of circumstance, having received high missions in poor markets, had a stretch of bad luck, or both.

To probe this possibility further, monthly predictions of success probabilities were generated for each sample observation (station-month) using the estimates reported in Table 3.2. Given those predictions,

Table 3.10
Frequency of Regular Army Mission Success:
Comparison of Actual and Predicted Rates

Number of Successes in Six Months	Actual Frequency	Predicted Frequency*
0	16.18%	10.21%
1	24.60%	24.48%
2	23.75%	29.42%
3	17.64%	21.97%
4	10.54%	10.46%
5	5.33%	3.03%
6	1.97%	0.41%

*The predicted frequency for the 2001–2003 period was computed from the probability of making the RA mission box using the logistic model reported in Table 3.2.

the probability distributions for numbers of successes during six-month windows were computed. The simulation provides the expected number of stations achieving success in a six-month period, accounting for differences in the level of the mission, the quality of the market, and the month-to-month values for all 56 independent variables included in the model. The predicted frequencies are presented in the second column of Table 3.10.

Since the logistic model does not account for cross-station differences in leadership, ability, or effort, the wedge between the actual and predicted distribution can be viewed as being reflective of these (and other) unmeasured factors. So, for example, the model predicts that 0.41 percent of stations will be successful during six of six months and 3.03 percent will succeed in five of six months. The actual frequencies for these two categories were 1.97 percent and 5.33 percent, respectively. In other words, one would conclude that about half of the highly successful recruiters were merely fortunate.

At the other extreme, the predicted frequency of stations with no successes in a six-month period is 10.21 percent, compared with an actual percentage of 16.18 percent. Thus, over 60 percent of such stations are unlikely to be poor performers in the future, especially if missions are set at levels reflecting local market quality.

Table 3.11 examines performance windows of different lengths. In particular, consider actual and predicted probabilities of failing to make mission in one month, in two consecutive months, and from 3 to 18 consecutive months.[18] Over 64 percent of all stations failed to make mission in a single month based on observable market, station, and mission characteristics. Over a two-month window, about 46 percent of stations fail twice, but the model predicts only 42 percent. In other words, about 91 percent of the two-time failures (last column) are

---

[18] The respective probabilities for six consecutive failures differ slightly from those reported in Table 3.10 due to sample differences. Table 3.10 includes all stations that appeared in the sample for at least 6 consecutive months. The sample described in Table 3.11 includes a smaller set of stations that appeared in the sample for at least 18 consecutive months. Stations that perform poorly are more likely to be closed down, and, therefore, some of these stations do not appear in the 18-month sample. Thus, the probabilities of failure are slightly lower in this group.

Table 3.11
Chronic Failure to Make Regular Army Mission
as a Measure of Performance

Consecutive Months of Failure	(A) Actual	(B) Predicted	(B)/(A) % Predicted
1	64.54%	64.35%	99.70%
2	46.33%	41.99%	90.63%
3	33.90%	27.79%	81.96%
4	25.73%	18.57%	72.17%
5	20.11%	12.57%	62.47%
6	15.81%	8.63%	54.59%
7	12.78%	6.02%	47.14%
8	10.27%	4.20%	40.90%
9	8.23%	2.94%	35.72%
10	6.67%	2.05%	30.78%
11	5.44%	1.44%	26.45%
12	4.42%	1.01%	22.88%
13	3.64%	0.72%	19.73%
14	2.95%	0.51%	17.25%
15	2.39%	0.36%	15.08%
16	1.94%	0.25%	13.13%
17	1.57%	0.18%	11.56%
18	1.25%	0.13%	10.44%

expected given observable station-level factors. As the window lengthens, the proportion of stations identified as chronic failures diminishes. Moreover, one can be more confident that the stations that continue to fail are, in fact, relatively poor performers. For example, only 1.25 percent of the stations actually failed every single month during an 18-month period. However, one would expect such extreme failure only 0.13 percent of the time. Thus, about 90 percent of those who might be identified as poor performers because they fail 18 months in a row actually are.

If this 18-month standard were adopted for screening purposes, it would be relatively fair, but not very effective, because it selects only about 1.25 percent of the stations. Moreover, by the end of an 18-

month period, the tours of duty for many recruiters at these stations will have ended or will be nearing completion. A six-month standard has a greater impact in terms of identifying larger numbers of poor performers, but about half of the low-performing group may, in fact, merely be unlucky recruiters faced with relatively difficult missions.

In sum, the evidence presented in this chapter suggests that the mission process during the 2001–2003 period was imperfect from an equity perspective because mission allocations did not adequately control for systematic differences in market and station factors that affect enlistment outcomes. Furthermore, success or failure in meeting mission can be a poor predictor of future productivity. Of course, there are efficiency concerns as well. Perceptions of fairness are likely to affect morale and recruiter effort.[19]

Also, to the extent that a performance target is either unrealistic or unchallenging, effort can be affected. Such efficiency issues are emphasized in Chapters Four and Five.

_____

[19] See, for example, Darmon (1997).

CHAPTER FOUR

Station Missions, Market Quality, Recruiter Effort, and Production of High-Quality Contracts

There is good reason to expect that missions, when effectively allocated, can induce increased recruiter effort and promote more efficient use of recruiting resources.[1] In this chapter we develop a new model of recruiter behavior and estimate the parameters of that model using the station-level data described and analyzed in Chapter Three.

Inducing Effort: Lessons from Private-Sector Literature

A critical consideration in recruiter productivity is recruiter effort. To be highly productive, recruiters must work hard and work smart. High and sustained levels of effort will result only if recruiters are motivated to succeed, high levels of effort are required to succeed, and high levels of effort give recruiters a good chance to succeed.[2] In the private sector, success is often defined in terms of performance relative to tangible sales quotas. The Army's version of quotas or goals is missions.

A key motivation for our analysis is that many recruiters, as well as many in the Recruiting Command hierarchy, believe that many stations are assigned missions that are consistently too high or too low given the potential or quality of their local recruiting markets. For example, it is widely believed that missions can be consistently achieved without

---

[1] See, for example, the meta-analysis of Tubbs (1986).

[2] See, for example, the discussion of "expectancy theory" in Chowdhury (1993, p. 29).

high levels of effort—i.e., missions are too easy—for some stations. A symptom of this is the adage: "Make mission, go fishin'." Moreover, there is reason to believe that other stations often have missions that can rarely be achieved even with very high levels of effort—i.e., missions are too difficult—which is suggested by not-uncommon statements such as "No one has ever boxed in that station." Where missions are too easy, the Army should expect that some recruiters will respond by not putting forth high levels of effort, and potential overproduction possibilities will be lost. Where missions are too hard, some recruiters may become discouraged and not put forth high levels of effort.[3]

The basic problem is easier to describe than to solve. Evidence presented in Chapter Three indicates that market quality varies considerably more from station to station than do missions. Market quality varies over stations for many reasons, such as differences in QMA, propensity to enlist in the military, reputation of the Army relative to the other services, quality of employment opportunities for high-quality high school graduates, and costs of attending local colleges.

Microeconomic Models of Mission Difficulty, Recruiter Effort, and Station Productivity

In this section we present and analyze mathematical models to (a) provide a foundation for our empirical work, (b) consider rules for allocating national-level missions across stations to maximize high-quality enlistments, and (c) analyze potential conflicts between efficiency (maximizing high-quality enlistments) and equity across recruiters.

In particular, we propose a theoretical framework that explicitly models recruiter effort and the quality of a station's market and then

---

[3] See, for example, hypothesis H_1 in Chowdhury (1993, p. 31), who conducts experiments that provide empirical support for declining effort when task difficulty becomes sufficiently high (e.g., Chowdhury, 1993, Figure 3, p. 36). A mechanism that could underlie such behavior is suggested by "expectancy theory." In particular, effort is predicted to decline with increased sales quotas when these quotas are "very high" if extra effort is perceived not to increase the likelihood of succeeding or the "expectancy of task success" (Chowdhury, 1993, pp. 29–31). See also Darmon (1997).

combines them to develop a model determining the expected number of high-quality enlistments in a particular station in a particular month. The key ideas are:

- The amount of effort expended by a recruiter depends on the difficulty of achieving his or her enlistment goal.
- The difficulty of achieving an enlistment goal depends on the goal and the quality of the market area assigned to the recruiter's station.
- When difficulty is low, increasing difficulty will increase effort.
- If difficulty is very high, increasing difficulty may decrease effort.
- The expected number of enlistments for a station in a particular month depends on the quality of the market and the total effort expended by the station's on-production recruiters.

As will be seen, according to the models introduced presently, the existence of a conflict between efficiency and equity in assigning missions depends on whether recruiters in all stations systematically respond in the same manner to changes in the difficulty of achieving recruiting goals.

In Model I, all stations are assumed to have the same *effort function*, namely the function that maps the difficulty of a station's high-quality mission into effort expended per recruiter. The analysis of Model I shows that for an *efficient* (i.e., expected-contract-maximizing) allocation of the national-level contract mission across stations, difficulty per recruiter is equalized across all stations. Thus, in this model, there is no conflict between equity and efficiency.

Model II is identical to Model I except that it generalizes Model I by allowing the effort function to differ across the stations. The analysis of Model II shows that for an efficient allocation of the national-level contract mission across stations, difficulty per recruiter is *not* equalized across all stations. Thus, in this model, there is a conflict between equity and efficiency.

Model I: Effort Functions Are Identical Across Stations

Consider a set of recruiting stations, indexed by s, in a given month, and let[4]

c_s = high-quality (HQ) contracts signed in station s

m_s = the high-quality mission

l_s = high-quality DEP loss charged that month

$g_s \equiv m_s + l_s$ = high-quality enlistment *goal* in station s

N_s – number of OPRA recruiters in station s

e_{is} = effort level of each OPRA recruiter i in station s[5]

$e_s = N_s e_{is}$ = total effort by all OPRA recruiters in station s

c_s^* = quality of the market in the recruiting area of station s

We define the quality of a station's market (c_s^*) as the marginal product of recruiter effort in producing high-quality contracts in that area. This definition formalizes the idea that what makes one station's market better than another's is that it is easier to enlist high-quality youths in the former station's assigned geographical area (alternatively, effort is more productive in better markets).

In particular, we assume that the expected number of high-quality contracts signed in station s is given by

$$Ec_s = c_s^* e_s,   \tag{1}$$

which formalizes the ideas that contracts increase with both effort and market quality, and that these factors are mutually reinforcing. Equa-

---

[4]   For economy of notation, we suppress the month index throughout this chapter.

[5]   We assume that in a given month every OPRA recruiter in a station expends the same level of effort.

tion (1) also assumes that c_s^* is the average product of recruiter effort for station s as well as the marginal product.[6] Rearranging (1) yields

$$e_s = Ec_s / c_s^*, \tag{2}$$

which shows that the effort required from all recruiters in a station to achieve a given level of expected contracts is inversely proportional to c_s^*.

During the period we study empirically, January 2001 through June 2003, missions were assigned at the station level, and station commanders may or may not have assigned specific goals (that we cannot observe) to individual recruiters. Nonetheless, because the management and psychology literature on goal difficulty and effort pertains to individuals, it is helpful to formalize the concept of a recruiter's difficulty in meeting his or her high-quality goal. To do so, consider a station with N_s recruiters on production, monthly goal equal to g_s, and market quality equal to c_s^*. For that station's expected contracts to equal g_s, (2) implies that total effort by all OPRA recruiters must be $e_s = g_s / c_s^*$. Thus the average effort required per recruiter is $e_{is} = (g_s / N_s) / c_s^*$. Accordingly, we define the difficulty facing recruiter i in station s (d_{is}) as

$$d_{is} = \frac{g_s / N_s}{c_s^*}, \tag{3}$$

---

[6] To elaborate, equation (1) assumes that the production function mapping effort to expected contracts is linear. This strong assumption assumes away the possibility that a station's effort in a single month is high enough to begin to deplete the pool of potential enlistees in a station area in a given month. (Stated differently, the assumption is that the marginal product of effort is constant for effort levels over the ranges of effort expended during the station-month pairs contained in our data.) We believe the assumption is appropriate because it greatly simplifies the analysis, and that this first attempt to separate empirically effort and market quality should be based on the simplest plausible model that can achieve that separation. Ultimately, the utility of this assumption is an empirical question, and we view generalization of the approach to allow for more flexible production functions as an important issue for further research.

which can be interpreted as the level of effort required of each recruiter to achieve the monthly station goal in expectation, given the quality of the station's market area.

Finally, we assume that effort per recruiter depends on the difficulty faced by each recruiter, and is given by the *effort function*:

$$e_{is} = f(d_{is}), \tag{4}$$

with effort initially increasing but perhaps eventually decreasing in difficulty. Formally, we assume that $f' > 0$ for sufficiently small (d_{is}), and $f'' < 0$ throughout.

Contract-maximizing missions under Model I. Here we consider efficient choices of missions, i.e., missions chosen to maximize the expected number of high-quality enlistments at the national level. In analyzing allocation of missions, we ignore DEP losses and focus on missions rather than goals, because missions are assigned on a quarterly basis, and the levels and locations of future DEP losses are unpredictable to USAREC at the time that they assign missions.

For expositional convenience, we assume that USAREC assigns missions at the station level.[7] We assume throughout that when assigning missions, USAREC knows the number of OPRA recruiters who will be on duty each month and the quality of the market area for each station (formally, we assume that USAREC knows $\{N_s, c_s^*\}$ for all stations).

First, consider "bottom-up" determination of station-level missions, i.e., assigning missions to each station to maximize expected high-quality enlistments station by station. The solution to this problem is to assign missions to each station so that effort is maximized for every station, or equivalently that $\partial Ec_s / \partial m_s = 0$ for all stations.

However, USAREC actually assigns missions through a top-down process. The first step is to determine the total national-level

---

[7]   In reality, USAREC assigns missions to brigades and recommends missions for battalions, and the allocations of missions below the brigade level are determined by brigades, battalions, and companies.

high-quality contract mission, which we denote by M.[8] The second step is to allocate this total to individual recruiting stations. Thus, we assume that USAREC knows $\{N_s, c_s^*\}$ for s = 1, 2, . . . , S and chooses a set of missions $\{m_s\}$ satisfying

$$M \equiv \sum_{s=1}^{S} m_s$$

to maximize the expected number of contracts at the command level, which is given by[9]

$$EC \equiv \sum_{s=1}^{S} Ec_s .$$

Using (1), (3), and (4), the Lagrangian for this constrained maximization problem is[10]

$$L = \sum_s c_s^* N_s f(m_s / N_s c_s^*) + \lambda \left(M - \sum_s m_s \right), \qquad (5)$$

where λ is the Lagrange multiplier associated with the constraint on the total mission.

The necessary (first-order) conditions for an optimum (with positive missions for all stations) are

$$\frac{\partial L}{\partial m_s} = c_s^* N_s f'(d_{is}) \frac{1}{c_s^* N_s} - \lambda = f'(d_{is}) - \lambda = 0 \quad \forall s \qquad (6a)$$

and

---

[8]   The national-level contract mission is determined on the basis of projected force requirements, availability of space in training classes, and projected rates of DEP loss.

[9]   We assume throughout our analyses of Models I and II that the national-level, high-quality contract mission (M) is feasible in the sense that M is no greater than the maximum achievable value of national-level expected high-quality contracts (EC).

[10]   All summations are over s = 1, 2, . . . , S, where S is the total number of stations.

$$\frac{\partial L}{\partial \lambda} = M - \sum_s m_s = 0 .$$ (6b)

Equations (6a), which are S in number, imply that $f'(d_{is}) = \lambda \; \forall s$.[11] With $f'' < 0$, as we have assumed, we conclude that a contract-maximizing allocation of missions equalizes mission difficulty per recruiter across all stations (as well as equalizing $\partial Ec_s / \partial m_s$ across all stations).[12] In this model, then, there is no conflict between efficiency (i.e., maximizing the expected number of contracts) and equity in terms of the difficulty of making mission.[13]

To derive expressions for the efficient missions, which we denote by $\{m_s^*\}$, we proceed as follows. Since at an optimum difficulty is equalized across stations, $\{m_s^*\}$ must satisfy

$$\frac{m_s^*}{c_s^* N_s} = k$$

for all s, or $m_s^* = k c_s^* N_s$ for all s. Summing the latter expression over s yields

$$M = \sum_s m_s^* = k \sum_s c_s^* N_s ,$$

---

[11] This means that at an optimum, missions are allocated so that the slope of the effort function is equalized across stations.

[12] The derivations assume that the solution is symmetric across stations. Strictly, this may ignore preferable strategies. For example, suppose that the command-level mission is higher than the sum of the optimal bottom-up missions, in which case $EC \geq M$ is infeasible. Then the best top-down strategy is to mission $S - 1$ of the stations at effort- and contract-maximizing levels and overmission the station with the lowest number of expected contracts given maximal effort (possibly to an absurd degree) to satisfy the constraint on total missions. We view the symmetry assumption as reflecting an implicit constraint to guard against such extreme inequities across stations.

[13] Note, however, that without further assumptions, we cannot rule out the possibility that efficient missions are not equitable across recruiters in terms of other attractive criteria for equity, such as equalizing the probability of making mission, which is the criterion for equity used in our analyses in Chapter Three.

or

$$k = \frac{M}{\sum_s c_s^* N_s},$$

which implies the optimal missioning rule:

$$m_s^* = \frac{c_s^* N_s}{\sum_s c_s^* N_s} M. \tag{7}$$

This rule means that a station's share of the national mission should be set equal to its share of the total national $c_s^* N_s$. To develop intuition about this rule, recall that $Ec_s = c_s^* e_s$ (from equation (1)) and $e_s = N_s e_{is}$, which imply $Ec_s = c_s^* N_s e_{is}$. This last expression implies that if effort per recruiter were equalized over all recruiters nationally, then expected contracts for each station would be proportional to its $c_s^* N_s$, or market quality multiplied by the number of OPRA recruiters. Thus, the rule given by (7) is that each station's mission should be the national mission multiplied by the station's share of the national total of expected high-quality enlistments if all OPRA recruiters in all stations were to expend the same level of effort.

Model II: Effort Functions Differ Across Stations
The assumption that effort functions are identical across stations is restrictive. For example, we might expect that effort depends on recruiter morale in addition to the difficulty of achieving the monthly goal for high-quality enlistments. Thus, if morale varies across stations, we might expect that for any level of difficulty that is constant across stations, effort per recruiter will be higher for stations with better morale.

Here we show that if effort functions do differ across stations, then it will generally not be efficient (i.e., expected-contract-maximizing) to equalize difficulty across recruiters. Thus, there generally is a conflict between equity and efficiency in setting missions.

To see this, assume that the effort function in (3) has a parabolic form and that the parameters of this function differ across stations:

$$e_{is} = 1 + \beta_s d_{is} + \gamma_s (d_{is})^2 .\tag{8}$$

Then, (1), (3), and (8) imply

$$\begin{aligned} Ec_s &= c_s^* N_s e_{is} = c_s^* N_s (1 + \beta_s d_{is} + \gamma_s (d_{is})^2) \\ &= c_s^* N_s + \beta_s g_s + \gamma_s \frac{g_s^2}{c_s^* N_s} . \end{aligned}\tag{9}$$

Proceeding as we did above for Model I, in the interest of efficiency, USAREC should choose $\{m_s\}$ to maximize command-level expected high-quality contracts[14]

$$EC \equiv \sum_s Ec_s = \sum_s [c_s^* N_s + \beta_s m_s + \gamma_s \frac{m_s^2}{c_s^* N_s}]$$

subject to the constraint $\sum_s m_s = M$.

The Lagrangian for this problem is

$$L = \sum_s [c_s^* N_s + \beta_s m_s + \gamma_s \frac{m_s^2}{c_s^* N_s}] + \lambda \left(M - \sum_s m_s \right),$$

with first-order conditions

$$\frac{\partial L}{\partial m_s} = [\beta_s + \frac{2\gamma_s m_s}{c_s^* N_s}] - \lambda = 0 \quad \forall s\tag{10a}$$

---

[14] Again, this analysis ignores DEP losses and focuses on missions rather than goals.

and

$$\frac{\partial L}{\partial \lambda} = M - \sum_s m_s = 0 . \qquad (10b)$$

Equations (10a) and (10b) imply that (a) $\partial Ec_s / \partial m_s$ is equalized across stations, and (b)

$$m_s^* = \frac{(\lambda - \beta_s)c_s^* N_s}{2\gamma_s} \quad \forall s .$$

It follows that

$$M = \sum_s m_s = \sum_s \frac{(\lambda - \beta_s)c_s^* N_s}{2\gamma_s} = \lambda \sum_s \frac{c_s^* N_s}{2\gamma_s} - \sum_s \frac{\beta_s c_s^* N_s}{2\gamma_s},$$

and rearranging implies

$$\lambda = \frac{M + \sum_s \dfrac{\beta_s c_s^* N_s}{2\gamma_s}}{\sum_s \dfrac{c_s^* N_s}{2\gamma_s}} .$$

Substituting this expression into

$$m_s^* = \frac{(\lambda - \beta_s)c_s^* N_s}{2\gamma_s} = (\lambda - \beta_s)\frac{c_s^* N_s}{2\gamma_s} \quad \forall s$$

yields the missioning rule,

$$m_s^* = \left(\frac{M + \sum_s \dfrac{\beta_s c_s^* N_s}{2\gamma_s}}{\sum_s \dfrac{c_s^* N_s}{2\gamma_s}} - \beta_s \right) \frac{c_s^* N_s}{2\gamma_s}, \tag{11}$$

and difficulty per recruiter in station s is given by

$$d_{is} = m_s^* / N_s c_s^* = \left(\frac{M + \sum_s \dfrac{\beta_s c_s^* N_s}{2\gamma_s}}{\sum_s \dfrac{c_s^* N_s}{2\gamma_s}} - \beta_s \right) \frac{1}{2\gamma_s},$$

which clearly differs over s.

Econometric Specifications

Using this theoretical model as a foundation, the goal is to estimate the determinants of monthly high-quality contracts at the station level, which we denote by y_s. Combining equations (1), (3), and (4) yields an expression for expected high-quality contracts signed by station s in a particular month:

$$E y_s = E c_s = c_s^* N_s e_{is}. \tag{12}$$

However, both c_s^* (station-level market quality) and e_{is} (effort per recruiter in station s) are unobservable. We relate these concepts to measurable variables as follows.

Assume that the marginal (and average) product of recruiter effort for station s in a particular month is linearly related to observable variables contained in the vector x_s:

$$c_s^* = \alpha' x_s. \tag{13}$$

Assume further that the effort function for a recruiter is parabolic, specializing (8) so that the parameters of the effort function depend on an observable variable denoted by z_s:

$$e_{is} = 1 + (\beta + \beta_1 z_s) d_{is} + (\gamma + \gamma_1 z_s)(d_{is})^2, \tag{14}$$

where (as above)

$$d_{is} = \frac{g_s / N_s}{c_s^*}$$

is the difficulty facing a recruiter in station s of signing his or her share of the station-level high-quality mission. Note that as long as z_s varies over s, (14) specializes to identical effort functions for all stations if and only if $\beta_1 = 0$ and $\gamma_1 = 0$.

Higher levels of z_s may, for example, be indicative of higher morale and more confidence in their abilities among recruiters in station s. In the empirical work, we assume that morale or confidence in a particular station depends on its recent, past performance in signing high-quality youths relative to the station's high-quality mission.[15] In our empirical implementation of this model, we measure a station's recent, past performance by that station's total high-quality enlistments divided by its total high-quality mission over the twelve-month period ending three months before the current month. (This is the variable R defined in Table 3.1.) Equation (14) assumes (as in equation (8)) that the intercept

---

[15] A mechanism that may underlie a positive link from a higher degree of past success to higher current effort, other things equal, is discussed in Chowdhury (1993), who presents supporting experimental evidence. The key concept is "self-efficacy," which "refers to a person's perception of his or her own level of mastery within a limited task domain." Higher self-efficacy is expected to increase "an individual's own estimate of the probability of task success (i.e., subjective expectancy)," and, as a result, "contribute to increases in effort expended." (Chowdhury, 1993, p. 31.) For discussion of the potential effects of past performance relative to sales quotas on morale and future performance, see, for example, Darmon (1997).

of the effort function equals one. This is a normalization imposed in estimation. A normalization is required to resolve a fundamental indeterminacy between e_{is} and c_s^*. In particular, because e_{is} and c_s^* are both unobservable and have no natural scales, their scales are arbitrary, as can be seen by noting from (12) that we could (for example) double the scale for one and halve the scale of the other and these two sets of scales would have the same implications for observables. The normalization resolves this ambiguity.

Note further that

$$\frac{\partial e_{is}}{\partial d_{is}} = (\beta + \beta_1 z_s) + 2(\gamma + \gamma_1 z_s)(d_{is}),$$

so effort first increases and then decreases with increasing difficulty, as the literature leads us to expect, if $(\beta + \beta_1 z_s) > 0$ and $(\gamma + \gamma_1 z_s) < 0$. Moreover, if $(\beta + \beta_1 z_s) > 0$ and $(\gamma + \gamma_1 z_s) < 0$, effort is maximized, i.e.,

$$\frac{\partial e_{is}}{\partial d_{is}} = 0,$$

when difficulty is $d_{is} = \dfrac{-(\beta + \beta_1 z_s)}{2(\gamma + \gamma_1 z_s)}$, which is positive.

To derive an expression for expected contracts that is amenable to estimation, substitute (13) and (14) into (12), use

$$d_{is} = \frac{g_s / N_s}{c_s^*},$$

and rearrange:

$$Ey_s = Ec_s = c_s^* N_s [1 + (\beta + \beta_1 z_s) \frac{g_s / N_s}{c_s^*} + (\gamma + \gamma_1 z_s)(\frac{g_s / N_s}{c_s^*})^2]$$

$$= (\alpha' x_s) N_s + (\beta + \beta_1 z_s) g_s + (\gamma + \gamma_1 z_s)(\frac{g_s^2}{(\alpha' x_s) N_s}).$$

$$(15)$$

The parameters of (15) are $(\beta, \beta_1, \gamma, \gamma_1, \alpha)$, which are the parameters of the effort function and the relationship between market quality and observable station-level characteristics. In the empirical work, we append an additive disturbance to (15) and estimate these parameters by nonlinear least squares.

To interpret (15), note that $\dfrac{\partial g_s}{\partial m_s} = 1$ and calculate

$$\frac{\partial Ec_s}{\partial m_s} = \frac{\partial Ec_s}{\partial g_s}\frac{\partial g_s}{\partial m_s} = \frac{\partial Ec_s}{\partial g_s} = (\beta + \beta_1 z_s) + 2(\gamma + \gamma_1 z_s)d_{is}, \quad (16)$$

which may be positive or negative depending on the values of parameters of the effort function, namely $(\beta, \beta_1, \gamma, \gamma_1)$. In particular,

$$\frac{\partial Ec_s}{\partial m_s} > 0$$

if and only if $\beta + \beta_1 z_s > -2(\gamma + \gamma_1 z_s)d_{is}$, which is equivalent to

$$\frac{\partial e_{is}}{\partial d_{is}} = (\beta + \beta_1 z_s) + 2(\gamma + \gamma_1 z_s)(d_{is}) > 0.$$

Thus, increasing the mission will increase expected contracts if and only if the increase in difficulty increases recruiter effort.

To interpret the elements of α, the vector of coefficients of the variables assumed to determine market quality, let α_j and x_j denote the jth elements of the vectors α and x_s, respectively. Note that (15) can be written as

$$Ec_s = c_s^* N_s + (\beta + \beta_1 z_s)g_s + (\gamma + \gamma_1 z_s)(\frac{g_s^2}{c_s^* N_s}),$$

and thus the (partial) effect of increasing x_j on expected contracts is given by

$$\frac{\partial Ec_s}{\partial x_j} = \frac{\partial Ec_s}{\partial c_s^*}\frac{\partial c_s^*}{\partial x_j} = \left[N_s - (\gamma + \gamma_1 z_s)\left(\frac{g_s^2}{N_s c_s^{*2}}\right)\right]\alpha_j, \qquad (17)$$

which implies that $(\gamma + \gamma_1 z_s) < 0$ is sufficient (but not necessary) for $\mathrm{sgn}\left(\dfrac{\partial Ec_s}{\partial x_j}\right) = \mathrm{sgn}(\alpha_j)$.

Estimates and Interpretation

To estimate the parameters of (15), we used the station-level monthly data described in Table 3.1. The dependent variable is the number of high-quality contracts signed in each station-month. Missions were assigned at the station level for all stations during the sample period (January 2001 through June 2003). Table 4.1 details the variables included in the vector x_s and presents estimates for two econometric specifications that correspond to Models I and II discussed above. In particular, the first version imposes $\beta_1 = \gamma_1 = 0$ on equation (15), which implies that effort functions are identical across stations. The second version relaxes these constraints, and we freely estimate β_1 and γ_1 assuming that z_s in equation (15) equals R, the station's earlier high-quality production ratio. (The parameters α, β, and γ are freely estimated for both models.) Thus, we explore the possibility that effort functions depend on the degree of success relative to high-quality missions in the recent past.[16]

   Potential determinants of marginal productivity. Column B of Table 4.1 details the elements of the vector x_s, namely, the variables assumed to enter the c^* function defined by equation (13). These variables were introduced and described in Chapter Three, and Table 4.1 uses the same abbreviations of the variable names used in Table 3.1.

---

[16] We also considered alternative specifications, including different time periods in the past. We also used predictions of the probability of making mission based on the logistic models presented in Chapter Three. The model using the ratio R had the best fit, but the qualitative results from the alternative specifications were very similar.

Table 4.1
Nonlinear Least-Squares Regression Analyses of Monthly High-Quality
Contracts at the Station Level, January 2001 through June 2003

			Model I: Identical Effort Functions Across Stations		Model II: Effort Functions Vary with Recent Success	
A	B	C	D	E	F	G
Variable	Description	Para-meter	Coeff.	Std. Error	Coeff.	Std. Error
Effort Function:						
Q_t	High-quality goal	b	0.3620	0.0092	0.0242	0.0209
$Q_t * R$	Interaction, Goal * Ratio	b_1	0	*	0.4533	0.0194
Q_t^2	Goal squared	g	−0.0066	0.0013	0.0051	0.0054
$Q_t^2 * R$	(Goal squared) * Ratio	g_1	0	*	−0.0236	0.0061
Marginal Productivity Function:						
x_0	Intercept	a_0	−1.0384	0.1635	−0.6386	0.1667
x_1	2-recruiter station	a_1	−0.1195	0.0127	−0.1447	0.0162
x_2	3-recruiter station	a_2	−0.1536	0.0157	−0.1890	0.0182
x_3	4-recruiter station	a_3	−0.1990	0.0176	−0.2359	0.0200
x_4	5-recruiter station	a_4	−0.2060	0.0197	−0.2399	0.0219
x_5	6+ recruiter station	a_5	−0.2605	0.0241	−0.2851	0.0255
x_6	Reserve recruiters	a_6	0.2310	0.0152	0.1897	0.0157
x_7	Reserve mission, "other"	a_7	−0.0078	0.0131	−0.0195	0.0147
x_8	Reserve mission, prior service	a_8	−0.1278	0.0066	−0.0689	0.0101
x_9	Reserve mission, high school	a_9	−0.2546	0.0312	−0.2506	0.0317
x_{10}	DEP loss, "other" reserves	a_{10}	−0.0330	0.0168	−0.0236	0.0211
x_{11}	DEP loss, prior service reserves	a_{11}	0.1729	0.1559	0.0307	0.1424
x_{12}	DEP loss, high school reserves	a_{12}	0.1434	0.0166	0.0874	0.0159
x_{13}	Mission, "other" regular army	a_{13}	0.1479	0.0072	0.1456	0.0076
x_{14}	February	a_{14}	−0.0188	0.0140	−0.0100	0.0145
x_{15}	March	a_{15}	−0.0171	0.0138	−0.0279	0.0144
x_{16}	April	a_{16}	−0.0053	0.0143	−0.0210	0.0144

Table 4.1—continued

A	B	C	D	E	F	G
			Model I:		Model II:	
			Identical Effort Functions Across Stations		Effort Functions Vary with Recent Success	
Variable	Description	Parameter	Coeff.	Std. Error	Coeff.	Std. Error
x_{17}	May	a_{17}	−0.1093	0.0124	−0.1163	0.0142
x_{18}	June	a_{18}	0.1453	0.0158	0.1378	0.0156
x_{19}	July	a_{19}	0.1478	0.0160	0.1472	0.0161
x_{20}	August	a_{20}	0.0818	0.0160	0.0658	0.0162
x_{21}	September	a_{21}	0.0869	0.0160	0.1099	0.0160
x_{22}	October	a_{22}	0.1035	0.0149	0.1262	0.0151
x_{23}	November	a_{23}	0.0059	0.0135	0.0193	0.0148
x_{24}	December	a_{24}	0.0537	0.0153	0.0581	0.0156
x_{25}	Mountain	a_{25}	−0.0351	0.0157	−0.0789	0.0179
x_{26}	North Central	a_{26}	0.1150	0.0101	0.0293	0.0119
x_{27}	South	a_{27}	0.0737	0.0132	0.0389	0.0140
x_{28}	Pacific	a_{28}	−0.0121	0.0153	−0.0182	0.0162
x_{29}	Hot	a_{29}	0.00021	0.00004	0.00022	0.00004
x_{30}	Rain	a_{30}	−0.00002	0.00003	−0.00002	0.00003
x_{31}	Humidity	a_{31}	−0.0025	0.0003	−0.0020	0.0003
x_{32}	Commanders, on production	a_{32}	−0.2864	0.0182	−0.2469	0.0183
x_{33}	Recruiters on duty	a_{33}	0.3329	0.0324	0.3281	0.0362
x_{34}	Absent recruiter	a_{34}	0.2863	0.0161	0.2184	0.0156
x_{35}	Commanders, not on production	a_{35}	−0.2147	0.0312	−0.1296	0.0366
x_{36}	QMA per recruiter	a_{36}	0.0662	0.0067	0.0792	0.0071
x_{37}	Unemployment change	a_{37}	0.0562	0.0284	0.0878	0.0330
x_{38}	Unemployment level	a_{38}	0.1415	0.0085	0.0735	0.0103
x_{39}	Relative wage	a_{39}	−0.2078	0.0312	−0.1245	0.0313
x_{40}	Black	a_{40}	−0.4785	0.0333	−0.3531	0.0356
x_{41}	Hispanic	a_{41}	−0.1715	0.0242	−0.0675	0.0266
x_{42}	College	a_{42}	−0.0014	0.0008	−0.0011	0.0008

Table 4.1—continued

			Model I: Identical Effort Functions Across Stations		Model II: Effort Functions Vary with Recent Success	
A	B	C	D	E	F	G
Variable	Description	Para- meter	Coeff.	Std. Error	Coeff.	Std. Error
x_{43}	Urban population	a_{43}	0.0871	0.0234	0.0758	0.0252
x_{44}	Cluster population	a_{44}	0.0958	0.0399	0.0682	0.0416
x_{45}	Growth in single parent homes	a_{45}	0.0081	0.0013	0.0055	0.0012
x_{46}	Poverty	a_{46}	−10.9729	0.9055	−7.9138	1.0349
x_{47}	Catholic	a_{47}	−0.0431	0.0300	−0.0062	0.0360
x_{48}	Eastern religion	a_{48}	−0.8164	0.3967	0.2643	0.5473
x_{49}	Christian	a_{49}	0.1741	0.0622	0.2053	0.0596
x_{50}	Vet pop < 32	a_{50}	0.1214	0.1358	0.3114	0.1411
x_{51}	Vet pop 33–42	a_{51}	0.8503	0.0991	0.2955	0.1033
x_{52}	Vet pop 43–55	a_{52}	−0.6046	0.0492	−0.0262	0.0538
x_{53}	Vet pop 56–65	a_{53}	0.8310	0.0551	−0.0227	0.0616
x_{54}	Vet pop 65–72	a_{54}	−1.0841	0.0901	−0.1936	0.0928
x_{55}	Vet pop 73+	a_{55}	0.1483	0.0286	−0.0152	0.0280
x_{56}	Market share	a_{56}	0.0037	0.0004	0.0019	0.0004

Variables were included in the vector x_s if they were expected to help explain across-station variation in the marginal productivity of effort by OPRA recruiters in producing high-quality, regular Army enlistments. Some of these variables are characteristics of market areas that cannot be controlled by USAREC and, hence, may be interpreted as determinants of "market quality." How market-quality factors entered missioning procedures used by USAREC during our sample period defies simple description. (See the Addendum at the end of this chapter entitled "How Did USAREC Determine Missions During Our Sample Period?" for a discussion.) Other elements of x_s are not characteristics of markets and should be interpreted as determinants of the marginal productivity of recruiter effort that we hold constant in order to isolate the effects of market characteristics. For example, x_1

through x_5 are indicators of the number of OPRA recruiters on duty in a station during a sample month. These variables are included to control for any effects of station size on the marginal productivity of effort, and estimates of their coefficients in the c^* function may be useful in understanding how the productivity of effort depends on station size holding various other factors constant.

Estimated effort function and implications for enlistments. The parameter estimates and their standard errors are reported in the last four columns of Table 4.1. First consider the estimates of the effort function for Model II (top panel, columns F and G). Note, in particular, that the estimates of β_1 and γ_1 are highly statistically significant, with t-ratios for b_1 and g_1 of 23.36 and −3.87, respectively. This indicates that the hypothesis of identical effort functions can be confidently rejected.

Recalling (14), the estimated effort function is

$$e_{is} = 1 + (0.0242 + 0.453R)d_{is} + (0.0051 - 0.0236R)(d_{is})^2, \quad (18)$$

with derivatives with respect to difficulty given by

$$\partial e_{is}/\partial d_{is} = 0.0242 + 0.453R + 2(0.0051 - 0.0236R)d_{is} \quad (18a)$$

and

$$\partial^2 e_{is}/\partial d_{is}^2 = 2(0.0051 - 0.0236R). \quad (18b)$$

It follows that the estimated effort function has the inverted U-shape assumed to characterize the effort function (4) for almost all of our data points. This can be seen as follows. First, $\partial e_{is}/\partial d_{is} > 0$ if and only if

$$d_{is} < \frac{0.0242 + 0.453R}{-0.0102 + 0.0472R}.$$

Second, (18b) shows that $\partial^2 e_{is}/\partial d_{is}^2 < 0$ as long as $R > 0.216$, which is true for more than 99 percent of our sample. In summary, the estimated effort functions have the shape posited in the theoretical models on the basis of the literature on goal setting and effort in management and psychology.

To see what the estimated effort functions imply for the sensitivity of expected contracts to mission increases, consider the following. The estimates and (16) imply

$$\partial Ec_s / \partial m_s = \beta + \beta_1 z_s + 2(\gamma + \gamma_1 z_s)d_{is}$$
$$= (0.0242 + 0.453R) + 2(0.0051 - 0.0236R)d_{is}$$

and

$$\partial^2 Ec_s / \partial m_s^2 = \frac{2(\gamma + \gamma_1 z_s)}{N_s c_s^*} = \frac{2(0.0051 - 0.0236R)}{N_s c_s^*},$$

which is negative for almost all sample values of R. Thus, our estimates imply diminishing returns to enlistments from increasing missions.

Although the estimated curvature of the effort function allows for decreased effort as missions increase at high levels of mission difficulty, this was the case for only ten sample observations. In fact, the estimates suggest that recruiters would reduce effort only for levels of difficulty roughly ten times the average difficulty in the sample. These levels lie so far outside the range of observed data that they cannot be viewed as reliable estimates of likely effects. In sum, while there is strong evidence that the positive impact of mission increases on effort diminishes appreciably as difficulty increases, there is no evidence that during the sample period recruiters actually reduced effort in response to higher missions.[17]

---

[17] Because of this finding we considered another functional form for the effort function. More specifically, we estimated a version of the model using an exponential (rather than quadratic) form that allowed (depending on the values of its estimated parameters) effort to increase with difficulty at a decreasing rate, but never decrease no matter how high difficulty becomes. The implications of this specification were very similar to those reported here in terms of effects of mission increases on effort and the determinants of market quality.

Figure 4.1 plots, for three values of R, $\partial Ec_s / \partial m_s$ against the level of the station goal assuming that $N_s c_s^* = 1.67$, its sample mean. The values for R are 0.815, its sample mean, as well as 1.10 and 0.528, which are the mean plus and minus one standard deviation of R. The range of goals plotted (1.0 to 3.5) on the horizontal axis corresponds to the mean of Q_t (observed high-quality mission plus DEP loss, the empirical counterpart to g in the theoretical model) plus and minus one standard deviation.

As can be seen from the figure, differences in recent past performance (as measured by R) have substantial implications for the sensitivity of expected contracts to missions that operate through the sensitivity of effort functions to past performance. For example, for any value of the monthly goal, $\partial Ec_s / \partial m_s$ is almost twice as large for $R = 1.10$ than it is for $R = 0.528$. We interpret this result as indicating that stations with better morale or higher confidence, due to better recent

Figure 4.1
Derivatives of Expected Contracts with Respect to Goal for Three Levels of the Past Production Ratio

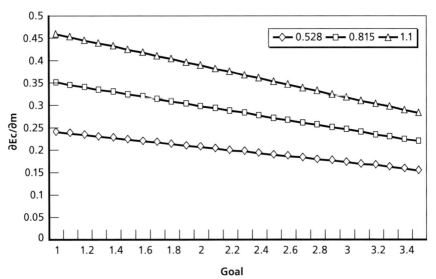

performance relative to their missions, are more responsive to increases in missions. This finding suggests that efficient missioning would take account of recent success by assigning higher missions to stations with better recent performance, all other things equal (such as number of recruiters and market quality). As we discuss below: (a) in assigning higher missions to stations that have been more successful recently, USAREC must be careful to avoid "punishing success," which could backfire by undermining morale; and (b) it appears that USAREC does exploit this opportunity, but to a lesser degree than appears appropriate.

Estimated determinants of marginal productivity. Now consider the estimates of the coefficients of the c_s^* function, i.e., the a_j reported in Table 4.1, which are the nonlinear least-squares estimates of the elements of the vector α in equation (13). We begin by noting that almost all of these estimates are highly statistically significant. In particular, 45 and 41 of the t-ratios for the 56 estimated slopes for the c_s^* function are significant at the 5 percent level for Models I and II, respectively. Moreover, the estimated coefficients differ in sign across the two models in only three of 56 cases, and in all three of these cases the estimate is not statistically significant for Model II. The values of a_j are also very highly correlated across the two specifications ($r = 0.985$). In discussing and interpreting the results concerning the c_s^* function, we emphasize those for the less-restrictive model that allows effort functions to vary across stations (Model II).

Figure 4.2 presents a histogram of estimated values of c_s^* for the sample observations. As can be seen from the figure, there is considerable variation in c_s^* across observations. For example, about 20 percent of the sample values are less than 0.4 and about 20 percent are more than 0.8. Thus, for the highest 20 percent of the station-months, effort is at least twice as productive than for the lowest 20 percent of the station-months. Second, the median estimated value of c_s^* is roughly 0.6, a value that provides a convenient benchmark for judging the sizes of various $\{a_j\}$.

Figure 4.2
Distribution of Estimated Marginal Products of Effort (c*)

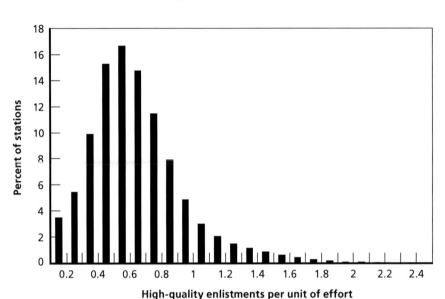

Recall that from (17) we concluded that $(\gamma + \gamma_1 z_s) < 0$ is sufficient (but not necessary) to imply that

$$\text{sgn}\ \frac{\partial E c_s}{\partial x_j} \quad - \quad \text{sgn}(\alpha_j) .$$

Our estimates imply $(\gamma + \gamma_1 z_s) < 0$ (for virtually all values of R). Thus, we interpret a positive (negative) value for a_j as implying that (according to our estimates) an increase (decrease) in x_j, other things equal, will increase (decrease) expected high-quality enlistments. We comment on the $\{a_j\}$ (estimates of $\{\alpha_j\}$) in the order they are presented in column F of Table 4.1.

Station size and numbers of recruiters. The estimated coefficients of x_1 through x_5 (the omitted category is stations with one OPRA recruiter on duty) are negative and increase in absolute value.

This pattern suggests that the marginal productivity of effort declines as station size increases. Moreover, given that the median value of c_s^* is roughly 0.6, the coefficients are very substantial. The total effect of an additional recruiter depends on the number of recruiters multiplied by c_s^*, so to compute the marginal effect of an additional recruiter on total enlistments, one has to account for all the interactions. On average, the marginal effect of adding one OPRA recruiter to a station would be an increase in average monthly high-quality enlistments of about one-half. This is about three-fourths of the average production per recruiter and implies that the marginal cost of producing an additional high-quality enlistment by adding recruiters is less than $6,000.

Army reserve recruiting. The next set of variables, x_6 through x_{12}, captures various features of the station's reserve recruiting operation, if any. In theory, the presence of on-production reserve recruiters in a station might increase or decrease the productivity of RA recruiter effort in signing high-quality, regular Army contracts. For example, reserve recruiting might help RA recruiting if reserve recruiters identify prospects who eventually sign RA contracts (positive spillovers). On the other hand, reserve recruiters might sign youths who would otherwise enlist in the regular Army (competition). On average, it appears that these effects cancel each other out. In particular, increases in reserve missions diminish RA contracts, holding the number of USAR recruiters constant, but an increase in the number of USAR recruiters, holding the reserve mission constant, confers positive spillover effects, and on average these effects sum to virtually zero. However, month-to-month and station-to-station variations in the reserve mission, the number of reserve recruiters, or both can have substantial productivity impacts, much as was evident for models of the probability of making mission discussed in Chapter Three.

Seasonal differences. Variables x_{14} through x_{24} indicate the month of the year and thus their coefficients capture differences in the productivity of recruiter effort due to seasonal differences in the propensity of high-quality youths to enlist and, perhaps, other factors such as advertising. The omitted category is January. Marginal productivity of OPRA recruiters is particularly high during the months of June, July, September, and October, with estimated coefficients (in Model

II) ranging from 0.11 to 0.15. The month of May appears to be a particularly bad month for signing high-quality youths, with a coefficient of -0.12. Compared with the median value of c_s^* of roughly 0.6, these seasonal differences are very considerable.

Regional differences. The estimated c^* function is also assumed to include the region of the country (x_{25} through x_{28}) because propensity to enlist is generally believed to vary considerably across regions. The omitted region is the Northeast. The estimated differences across regions are somewhat smaller than across months, with the Mountain region standing out as having relatively low marginal productivity of effort, other things equal.

Hometown climate. The next three variables, x_{29} through x_{31}, capture aspects of the summer climate in the station's geographic area. They are included because factors such as heat, rain, and humidity might affect youths' propensity to enlist and leave their hometown climate behind. The estimates suggest that propensity to enlist is higher in areas with hotter July temperatures (summer climates) and, surprisingly, lower in areas that are more humid in July.

Staffing. The next four variables, x_{32} through x_{35}, which are defined relative to the number of OPRA recruiters, are included to control for aspects of the regular Army recruiting force other than OPRA recruiters. The estimated coefficients for commanders on production (x_{32}) and (nonproduction) on-duty recruiters (x_{33}) largely offset each other.[18] The correlation between these indicator variables was extremely high. Specifically, when the data indicate the presence of a commander on production, the data almost always also indicate the presence of an on-duty (nonproduction) recruiter. Thus, while these variables seem useful as controls, their coefficients are difficult to interpret. The estimates suggest that when recruiters are assigned to a station but are not on production, station productivity increases. This might be the case if, for example, prospects the off-production recruiters had been working are signed during a month that the recruiters were not on production.

QMA and local economic factors. The next four variables, x_{36} through x_{39}, perform as expected. In particular, marginal productivity

---

[18] Specifically, the former coefficient is -0.2469 and the latter is 0.3281.

of recruiter effort is higher in areas where (a) more military-qualified youths are available per OPRA recruiter, (b) the unemployment rate is increasing, (c) the unemployment rate is higher, and (d) civilian wages are lower. The wage effects are of special interest because the station-level data, with large numbers of observations and significant wage variation from market to market, enable us to estimate them with more accuracy than has been possible in previous work using (more aggregated) data at the battalion or state level. The estimates indicate an average wage elasticity of 0.1365. This implies that the marginal cost of signing one additional high-quality recruit by raising military wages would be nearly $134,000.[19]

Demographic factors. Variables x_{40} through x_{49} represent a diverse set of demographic characteristics in the stations' recruiting areas. Unless otherwise noted, we expect that the estimated coefficients of these variables reflect differences in propensity to enlist, military qualifications, or both. The estimates suggest that recruiting productivity is lower in areas with (a) larger proportions of African Americans and Hispanics in the population, (b) larger proportions of youths attending college, (c) less urbanized populations,[20] (d) higher likelihood of a child being in a single-parent home in 2000 relative to 1990, (e) higher childhood poverty rates, (f) larger proportions of adherents to Eastern religions, and (g) smaller proportions of non-Catholic Christians.

Veteran populations. The next six variables (x_{50} through x_{55}) reflect the prevalence of veterans (of all services) in different age categories in 2001. We expect that these variables pick up the effects of unmeasured aspects of propensity to enlist that persist over long periods of time as well as the effects of veterans as youth influencers. The

---

[19] Simulations indicate that a 10 percent increase in the monthly military wage (from $1,500 to $1,650) would have an annual total cost of $5,346 for an average station that has to give the wage increase to all recruits (average of 2.971 enlistees per month times $150). In turn, the regression results indicate that the number of high-quality recruits rises by 0.04 due to the hypothesized wage increase. On a per-recruit basis, $5,346 divided by 0.04 yields a marginal cost of $133,698.

[20] This result may not be indicative of higher propensity in more urbanized areas but rather may reflect that recruiters have to travel longer distances to visit high schools, shopping malls, homes of prospects, etc., in less urbanized areas.

estimates indicate that recruiter effort is more productive in areas with more young veterans (aged less than 43 in 2001) but less productive in areas with more veterans between the ages of 56 and 65 in 2001. The latter result may represent lingering effects of negative experiences of military personnel during the Vietnam War era. Our results, then, conflict with the widespread view that veterans usually encourage youths to enlist (i.e., are "positive influencers"). Specifically, the results suggest a more nuanced view of the influence of veterans on the propensity of youth to enlist, namely, that the age composition of the local veteran population could be important.

Recent Army market share. The last variable, Army's share of total Department of Defense (DoD) contracts in the local area during 1999 (x_{59}), is expected to pick up any effects of a local preference for the Army and the strength of competition from the other services that persist over time. The estimated effect on the marginal productivity of effort is positive, as expected.

Relative importance of determinants of contracts and market quality. Which factors are most important in explaining differences across stations in high-quality enlistments? Which factors are most important in explaining differences across stations in market quality? Table 4.2 summarizes the results of calculations designed to explore these questions, providing information about the relative importance of groups of variables.

To compute the measures reported in Table 4.2, we used methods analogous to those described in Chapters Two and Three (see discussions of Tables 2.6, 3.4, and 3.6). Briefly, we multiplied estimated coefficients in Table 4.1 by the values of the corresponding explanatory variables in Table 4.1, summed these prediction contributions over the variables in each group, and computed standard deviations over all sample observations of these summed contributions. Such measures account for the magnitudes of the estimated coefficients as well as the amounts of sample variation in and co-variation among variables within each group. The results are reported in Table 4.2. For both contracts and c^*—which we refer to as "levels"—the relative importance of a group of variables is expressed as that group's percentage contribution to the sum of standard deviations for that level. So, for example, of the total sample variation in monthly, station-level contracts, just over half could be attributed to variations in mission and in DEP losses. Ranked in order of importance, variations in c^* are attributable to "other" RA missions, station size, monthly variations, etc.

Table 4.2
Sample Variation in Predicted Contracts and
Marginal Productivity of Effort Due to Groups of Factors

Category of Variables	Percent of Standard Deviation
Components of contracts:	
Mission	32%
DEP losses	20%
Recruiters × c*	48%
Components of c*:	**Percent of c* effect:**
Other missions	15%
Station size	13%
Monthly variations	12%
Demographics	10%
Reserves	9%
Market factors	8%
Regional differences	5%

NOTE: Subsets of variables described in the first column are named according to the groups of variables with corresponding names listed in Table 3.1 of which they are subsets. But these subsets include only those variables included in the regressions reported in Table 4.1.

Addendum

How Did USAREC Determine Missions During Our Sample Period?

During our data period of January 2001 through June 2003, USAREC used two very different approaches or models to incorporate market quality into the contract missioning process. In both cases, absolute missions were determined by rescaling relative brigade- and battalion-level missions as determined by a missioning model so that they would sum across recruiting units to command-level contract mission levels that were determined through a separate process. The first approach, which was used to determine quarterly missions from July 1999 through the first two quarters of calendar year 2001, was implemented using a model called "Brigade 80/20." The second approach that was used (albeit with various modifications) set missions in proportion to recruiter allocations as determined using a model called "RAM" (an acronym for "recruiter allocation model"). We describe these models in turn.

The "Brigade 80/20" model determined quarterly brigade-level missions in the three contract categories that were missioned separately (senior alpha, grad alpha, other) based on Army and total DoD (all four services) contract production levels during the previous three years. (There was no attempt to incorporate factors determining market quality in any direct fashion.) More specifically, for each of the five brigades: (a) the measure of Army contract production, which entered the model with a 20 percent weight, was Army, brigade-level contract production (in the same contract category) summed over the three previous corresponding calendar quarters; and (b) the measure of DoD contract production, which entered the model with a 80 percent weight, was DoD contract production (in the same contract category) during the past three years. The latter measure is considerably more important than the former for two reasons in addition to its 80 percent weight, namely (a) annual production levels are roughly four times larger than quarterly levels, and (b) Army contract levels were roughly 40 percent of corresponding DoD production levels. Thus, in the Brigade 80/20 model, the relative weight on past Army production was very small—roughly 2 percent (i.e., 0.20 × 0.25 × 0.40). Thus, missions determined using the Brigade 80/20 model we based almost entirely on DoD production levels over the previous three years. Besides the lack of any direct effect on missions of variables determining market quality, this fails to address even indirectly two issues that our econometric analysis is designed to take into account: (a) past production levels reflect both market quality and recruiter effort levels; and (b) the quality of a recruiting market for the Army may differ considerably from the quality of the market for the other three services.

Starting early in calendar year 2001, a new approach, imbedded in the RAM, was used to determine missions at the brigade level and recommended missions at the battalion level. The analysis was performed for station areas as well as zip codes. The description here focuses on determination for station areas. The RAM model determined missions according to six factors (with weights in the initial version in parentheses): (1) "potential contracts" (0.214), (2) projected 17- to 21-year-old population (0.222), (3) freshman and sophomore college population (0.172), (4) Army grad alpha market share in the previous fiscal year, adjusted so that this factor could not fall below a minimum level (0.139), (5) DoD-level, high-quality contract production over the previous three years (0.24), and (6) DoD-level, contract production of "others" (i.e., all but senior and grad alphas) over the previous three years (0.013). All six of these factors incorporate, directly or indirectly, aspects of market quality. The last three, which are based on past Army and DoD production, indirectly incorporate market quality but confound (as discussed with regard to the Brigade 80/20 model) market quality with past recruiter effort levels. The second and third factors are similar to some of the variables we use to estimate market quality for station areas and their determinants. Note, however, that—in contrast to our approach—these variables enter the RAM with preassigned weights that are not determined empirically by relating these variables to actual levels of contract production holding many other factors constant.

The first factor is an innovative approach to incorporating (albeit in an opaque manner) many demographic and economic factors that are explicitly incorporated (with their importance estimated empirically) in our econometric analysis. More specifically, the determination of "market potential" employs detailed, proprietary data from MicroVision's Household Lifestyle Segmentation System. This system allocates all U.S. households into one of 50 segments based on such factors as "family size, number and ages of children, income, property value, education levels, urban vs. suburban vs. rural, TV habits, music and magazine choices, types of leisure activities, retail purchasing patterns, etc." (Source: "MV50 Household Lifestyle Segmentation & Contract Production," one-page memo, USAREC, no date.) The market potential of each geographic area is determined by analyzing historical links between household segments and past (four-year) Army contract production levels to estimate penetration rates of Army enlistments by segment and then using current data on numbers of households in each segment for each station area. The potential usefulness of this approach is suggested by the fact that eleven of the 50 household segments accounted for 58 percent of Army contracts during the late 1990s. We do not have detailed information about how USAREC's missioning model changed from month to month to determine missions through the end of our sample period (June 2003), but it appears that factors and weights were adjusted fairly often. For example, as of early 2003, the weight on "market potential" had fallen to 0.12, and past Army and DoD production had total weights of 0.63.

Thus, models used at USAREC to determine missions for most of our sample period incorporated many of the same kinds of demographic and economic factors that we use explicitly in our econometric analysis to estimate determinants of market quality. How various demographic and economic factors contribute to market quality cannot, however, be gauged from available information. This is largely because the details of how demographic and economic information was used by MicroVision to define their 50 household segments are proprietary.

CHAPTER FIVE

Implications of Alternative Mission Policies for High-Quality Enlistments

In this chapter we examine whether USAREC could have improved productivity by changing the allocation of missions. First, we use the estimates from the last chapter (Model II) to predict or simulate the effects of various policies. Next, we assess the degree to which station productivity is predictable and whether there are gains to be made from a broader performance window, perhaps over several months or for larger organizational units.

Simulated Effects of Alternative Mission Policies

In Table 5.1, we provide summaries of nine policy options and their predicted effects. The last column of the table reports the predicted number of national high-quality enlistments during the sample period relative to that observed under the actual or status quo allocation of command-level high-quality missions.

The first three simulated policies (Policies I, II, and III) involve reallocation across stations of the actual number of command-level missions. These policies are based on shifting missions from station-months where the impact of mission is low (relatively low values of $\partial Ec_s / \partial m_s$, the sensitivity of expected contracts to missions) to station-months where the impact of mission is high (relatively large values of $\partial Ec_s / \partial m_s$). Under all three of these policies, each affected station-month has an increase or decrease of one mission.

Table 5.1
Policy Options for Changing Missions: Simulated Effects on High-Quality Contracts, January 2001 Through June 2003

Policy	Description	HQ Contracts Relative to Status Quo
Status quo	Actual total high-quality mission and allocation across stations	1.000
I	Reallocate 3,000 missions from low- to high-impact stations (15% of all stations)	1.010
II	Reallocate 10,000 missions from low- to high-impact stations (50% of all stations)	1.021
III	Reallocate 1 mission from half of the stations to the other half (32.5% of total mission)	1.027
IV	Remove DEP loss from goal and increase all stations' missions to maintain total goal	0.998
V	Allocate same mission to all recruiters in all months	1.009
VI	Allocate station missions in proportion to market quality (c*), on per-recruiter basis	1.007
VII	Increase monthly missions by 0.5 for all stations	1.057
VIII	Increase monthly missions by 1.0 for the half of stations with highest impact	1.074
IX	Increase mission using historic adjustment to past performance ratio	1.006

NOTE: Highest impact stations are those where the marginal increases in enlistments due to an increase in mission ($\partial Ec_s / \partial M_s$) are largest.

Under *Policy I*, 3,000 high-quality missions—representing about 2 percent of the total mission during the sample period—are reallocated from the 3,000 station-months with the smallest values of $\partial Ec_s / \partial m_s$ to those with the highest values. This reallocation affects about 15 percent of the sample station-months. As indicated in the last column of Table 5.1, this policy is predicted to increase contracts by only 1 percent relative to the status quo. That is, the ratio of the prediction for

Policy I to that for the status quo (actual allocation) is 1.010, which implies a 1 percent increase.[1]

Policy II involves the same general reallocation strategy as Policy I, but on a larger scale—10,000 missions (rather than 3,000). This more than tripling of the number of missions reallocated is predicted to increase contracts 2.1 percent relative to the status quo, or a bit more than twice the gain predicted for Policy I. The reason that increasing the scale of the reallocation more than threefold only doubles the improvement is that as more missions are reallocated, the spread between the values of $\partial Ec_s / \partial m_s$ between a pair of stations losing and gaining one mission declines as more missions are reallocated.

Policy III extends the strategy of Policies I and II to its logical extreme. In particular, it calls for a decrease of one mission for all station-months with $\partial Ec_s / \partial m_s$ below the median and a one-mission increase for all of the station-months above the median. This involves reallocating about 32.5 percent of the total mission. As reported in the table, Policy III is predicted to increase high-quality enlistments by 2.7 percent relative to the status quo.

Strictly, these estimates imply that we could reallocate more missions and increase enlistments. However, much of the variation in $\partial Ec_s / \partial m_s$ is due to differences in recent production (see Figure 4.1 and its discussion), and reallocating too much in this manner could result in undesirable dynamic effects (which are not captured in our

---

[1]   As we have seen (Figure 4.1 and its discussion), a large portion of the variation in the marginal impacts of increasing missions stems from the past performance ratio (R), the previous year's total high-quality contracts divided by total high-quality missions, lagged one quarter. Clearly, increased missions for the relatively successful stations would tend to diminish that ratio, because enlistments do not increase in proportion to the mission increases. In the long run, then, one might expect that a resulting narrowing of the distribution of R would diminish the value of the initial reallocation and, eventually, eliminate it. However, we have seen that a large portion of performance is due to either good or bad fortune. As a result, a high performance ratio for a station in one year far from guarantees a high ratio for that station in subsequent years. For example, a regression of a current year's ratio on the ratio one year earlier yields $R_t = 0.7606 + 0.0984\ R_{t-12}$. This suggests that the predicted production ratio for a station that had a ratio of 1.1 (one standard deviation above the mean of 0.85) is 0.88. For a station that had a ratio of 0.5, the prediction is 0.81. This suggests that additional opportunities for contract-increasing reallocations will continually emerge.

static model) if recruiters perceive that extra production will lead to higher future missions.

As discussed above, to have a chance to earn mission box points in a particular month, the number of high-quality contracts must be at least the station's high-quality mission in that month plus the number of high-quality DEP losses charged to the station in that month. *Policy IV* examines the effects of not holding individual stations accountable for DEP losses in this way. In particular, Policy IV eliminates DEP losses from each station's goal in every sample month and—to hold the aggregate goal constant—adds 0.44 to each station's mission, which is the average monthly high-quality DEP loss per station in our sample.[2]

This policy might seem desirable if recruiters do not have significant control over DEP losses and if an increase in uncertainty is demotivating. As we have seen, a DEP loss significantly impairs a station's probability of success and is a key factor in the monthly variation in the difficulty of mission facing individual stations (Tables 3.3, 3.4).

However, as reported in Table 5.1, this change in policy is predicted to reduce enlistments. This is because the primary factor that predicts a station's DEP losses is the size of the DEP, which tends to be higher the more successful the station was in the recent past. In other words, stations with high production ratios, for which the impact of a mission increase tends to be relatively high, tend to be the same stations that have the highest expected DEP losses. Thus, the current treatment of DEP loss is effective because it implicitly raises performance targets more for stations that have been relatively successful in the recent past.[3]

---

[2]   We also simulated a policy that anticipated that DEP losses would be higher for large stations with more enlistments, with missions increased by the same percentage for all stations. The results were qualitatively similar.

[3]   As reported in Table 5.1, the policies that directly allocate higher missions to high-impact stations (namely, Policies I, II, and III) are more effective and should be preferred. If the Army wishes to maintain incentives to manage DEP effectively, without affecting the marginal value of effort in the short run, it should be possible to do so by, for example, instituting large deductions in award points for DEP losses without changing the current contract level required to make mission.

The next policy we examine involves a very simple, albeit subopt-imal rule for allocating missions. In particular, *Policy V* assigns the same mission to all OPRA recruiters nationwide. To implement this policy would probably require a wider performance window (2 or 3 months, for example) because missions are small integers. However, such a policy would eliminate much of the month-to-month variation in mission that contributes to the variation in the marginal impact of mission increases. The estimates suggest that this could have improved performance slightly, by less than 1 percent.

Policy VI allocates missions per recruiter to stations in proportion to c_s^*, without regard to past performance. Although this method con-siders market difficulty in the allocation of mission, the most impor-tant element of differential impact according to our estimates—recent past recruiting success—is ignored.[4] Again, the results indicate some improvement, but the increase in high-quality enlistments is less than 1 percent.

Recall that our estimates imply that only a handful of the observed missions (specifically, 10) were so difficult that our estimates imply that they discouraged recruiters and led to reduced effort. Stated formally, the estimates imply that $\partial Ec_s / \partial g_s < 0$ for only 10 of the 42,000-plus station months. Thus, according to our estimates, increasing mis-sions across the board would have increased total enlistments over this time period. The next two policies explore the potential to increase enlistments by increasing the aggregate (command-level) mission by the same amount, but allocating the extra mission differently across stations. *Policies VII and VIII* involve increasing the high-quality mis-sion by one-half contract for all stations and by one contract for the half of the stations with the highest sensitivity of contracts to mission increases, respectively. The implied increase in total mission represents a 15.5 percent increase, since the mean of Q_m (monthly high-quality mission) is 3.20 (Table 3.1). Policies VII and VIII are predicted to

---

[4]   In fact, this allocation would be optimal if the effort functions were identical across sta-tions (see equation (7) in Chapter Four and its discussion), but our estimates indicate that the effort functions differ substantially according to the level of recent past success (Table 4.1).

increase contracts by 5.7 and 7.4 percent, respectively. Thus, the same increase in total mission, if strategically allocated (rather than evenly allocated) across stations, results in a 30 percent larger increase in contracts.[5] This result illustrates the large potential gains associated with effective allocation of missions generally and increases in missions in particular.

We emphasize that these results should *not* be interpreted to imply that increasing aggregate missions in today's recruiting environment would increase enlistments. This is because the difficulty of recruiting has changed dramatically since 2003, and, as a result, higher missions may be unachievable today, so raising missions could prove counterproductive.

All of the above policies that allocate missions using estimates of $\partial Ec_s / \partial m_s$ exploit, albeit to varying degrees, the dependence of the effort function on stations' recent performance. This general strategy involves higher missions for stations that have been more successful in terms of high-quality enlistments relative to high-quality mission. In fact, analysis of the station data from 2001 to 2003 indicates that USAREC did assign higher missions to stations that had higher production ratios in the past. Based on a regression, summarized in Table 5.2, that linked year-to-year changes in the high-quality mission to past performance ratios, we provide simulations for different levels of past success.[6] A station with a mean ratio (0.815) would experience no increase in mission. For ratios equal to the mean plus and minus two standard deviations, the mission changes were substantial. For the high-performing stations, missions were increased by almost 14 percent. The opposite was true of the low-performing stations.

According to this historical relationship, for a station with three recruiters, a mission adjustment of 0.4 or more was made for at most 5 percent of the sample station-months. This compares with a reallocation

---

[5] I.e., a 7.4 percent increase is almost exactly 30 percent larger than a 5.7 percent increase.

[6] The regression included monthly indicator variables and had an R-squared of 0.149. The estimated model was $Q_t / Q_{t-12} = a_t + 0.2392R$, where a_t is a time-specific intercept. The standard error of the slope estimate was 0.0065, indicating that this relationship is highly statistically significant.

Table 5.2
Historical Mission Adjustments Based on
Past Performance

Ratio	Percent Change in Mission	Change in Level of Mission
1.389	13.7%	0.41
1.102	6.9%	0.21
0.815	0	0.00
0.528	−6.9%	−0.21
0.241	−13.7%	−0.41

of 1 mission affecting every station under Policy III. Thus, it is not surprising that although USAREC's actual policy improved productivity, it fell well short of maximizing recruiting production through reallocation. Specifically, *Policy IX*, based on historic adjustments, yields 0.6 percent additional recruits, about 22 percent of the gains possible through Policy III, which involves more aggressive mission reallocation to recently successful stations.

Setting Mission in an Uncertain Environment

In Chapter Two, we saw that recruiter-level models were able to explain only a small portion of the variation in month-to-month production. Station-level models dramatically improved predictive ability, partially due to the availability of more appropriate market data and also because randomness is reduced when one sums over the multiple recruiters assigned to most stations. Despite this improvement, however, the station-level Model II described in Table 4.1 explains only about 40 percent of the variance in station-level production on a monthly basis.

This inability to predict contract outcomes accurately may reflect an inability to account for systematic differences over time or between stations. Or, it may be indicative of the random nature of the timing of decisionmaking when small numbers of youth are deciding whether to enlist in a given month. Each possibility may have different implications for missioning.

To better understand the station-level model's predictive ability, we generated model predictions over different time intervals and compared them with actual station-level enlistments. The results of simple regressions of actual contracts on predicted contracts are illustrated in Figure 5.1.[7] Clearly, the models do much better in predicting station performance over longer time intervals, which implicitly average randomness over more months. For the 12-month interval, the R-squared is 0.8123, only a bit more than that for 11-month intervals. In fact, most of the gain from aggregating the data over months occurs during the first three months, suggesting that if reducing uncertainty is an objective, a quarterly performance window could make sense. Moreover, if the goal of missioning is to equalize the difficulty of missions

Figure 5.1
Explaining High-Quality Enlistments over Multiple Months

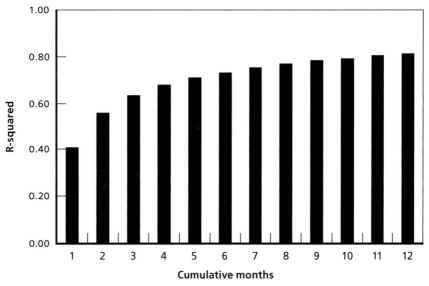

RAND *MG433-5.1*

---

[7] The computed R-squared statistics for different time intervals were derived by regressing the sum of monthly contracts on the sum of monthly predictions (based on Model II in Table 4.1) for individual stations.

over time, using the model developed in Chapter Four seems promising because it appears to account fairly well for variations in market quality.

In Chapter Two we saw that unobservable recruiter characteristics could account for as much as 10 percent of the individual variation in productivity. We also ran a regression of 12-month production on predicted enlistments, adding roughly 1,600 separate variables allowing for station-level fixed effects that could capture effects of unobserved market factors and abilities of station personnel. This model increased the predictive performance by about 0.10, reaching an R-squared of 0.9213.

CHAPTER SIX

Career Paths of Recruiters

This chapter examines the career histories of 88,000 enlisted personnel who entered the U.S. Army between 1987 and 1996. In a series of econometric analyses, the following three questions are addressed:

- Which enlisted personnel become recruiters, and what are their characteristics?
- How does becoming a recruiter affect the career trajectory of those selected?
- To what extent are recruiters rewarded for their productivity?

The answers to these questions will provide insights into some key human resource management issues. Namely, is the Army selecting the right soldiers to be recruiters? Are recruiters likely to be motivated to succeed? Are personal incentives well aligned with those of the organization?

The Enlisted Personnel Dataset

The data used for this analysis were drawn from the Enlisted Master File (EMF) that tracks career histories and personal characteristics of all individuals entering the Army during the ten-year period beginning in FY87. For the subset of individuals who served as recruiters during this time, information on productivity as recruiters, described in Chapter Two, was added to the file.

The analysis file contained records for only those soldiers who remained in the Army as of 2003.[1] About 30 percent of these soldiers had been in the Army for 10 or more years before becoming recruiters. Of this group, about half had reached rank E-6 and the other half E-7 by the time they became recruiters. Another 25 percent of recruiters had been in the Army only three to five years before joining the recruiting force, and the ranks of these soldiers were evenly split between E-5 and E-6 when they became recruiters.

Table 6.1 provides means and standard deviations for the sample, which includes both recruiters and nonrecruiters. Table 6.2 describes information specific to the 9,500 recruiters included in the study.

For each individual, career rank as of 2003 and time to promotion for the ranks of E-4 and E-5 were gathered.[2] As can be seen in Table 6.1, by 2003 almost 60 percent of the sample personnel (all of whom were still in the Army in 2003) had achieved E-6 and 14 percent had been promoted to the rank of E-7. Descriptive statistics for variables representing several personal characteristics are also reported in Table 6.1, including the presence of dependents, marital status, race, gender, performance on the AFQT, and education. Information on the primary occupational specialty was also included.

As can be seen from Table 6.1, about 10.5 percent of the individuals entering between 1987 and 1996 and serving at least until 2003 served as a recruiter sometime between 1997 and 2003. And, as reported in Table 6.2, about 15 percent of members of this subgroup served as recruiting station commanders at some time during this

---

[1] Since the research design relies heavily on comparisons between recruiters and nonrecruiters, sample selection was crucial. Clearly, any individual becoming a recruiter in the post-1997 period had to reenlist when his or her earlier terms of service had ended. On the other hand, a large percentage of the entering cohorts who did not become recruiters left the Army before 1997. Those returning to the private sector had systematically different profiles, on average. For example, they typically had slower promotion rates while in the Army. Thus, for most of the analyses, the sample included the 90,000 individuals remaining in the Army through 2003. The one exception is the analysis of separation between 2001 and 2003. In this case, the sample included 140,000 individuals who were still in the Army as of 2000.

[2] As shown in Hosek and Mattock (2003), speeds of promotion to these ranks (promotion speeds to lower ranks show almost no variation) provide information about a soldier's quality that is not captured by AFQT scores.

Table 6.1
Descriptive Statistics for Enlisted Personnel Career Histories

Variable	Definition	Mean	Standard Error
e6	Achieved rank E-6 as of 2003	0.5841	0.4929
e7	Achieved rank E-7 as of 2003	0.1409	0.3479
grade4	log(months to rank E-4)	3.3255	0.5113
grade5	log(months to rank E-5)	3.4568	0.5447
depend	Has dependent	0.6748	0.4685
marry	Married (0–1)	0.1953	0.3965
afqt	log (AFQT test score)	3.9967	0.3370
grad	High school graduate (0,1)	0.9870	0.1132
college	Attended college (0,1)	0.0906	0.2871
white	Race = white (0,1)	0.5271	0.4993
male	Gender = male (0,1)	0.8625	0.3444
Occupational Specialty:	Career Management Field codes (0,1)		
infantry	CMF 11, 18	0.1392	0.3462
armor	CMF 19	0.0523	0.2227
artillery	CMF 13, 14	0.0992	0.2990
signal	CMF 31	0.0532	0.2245
admin	CMF 46, 74	0.0791	0.2699
technical	CMF 51, 54, 77, 81	0.0791	0.2699
munitions	CMF 55	0.0553	0.2285
supply	CMF 76, 92	0.0082	0.0901
medical	CMF 91	0.0802	0.2716
police	CMF 95	0.0868	0.2815
food	CMF 94	0.0342	0.1817
intel	CMF 96	0.0218	0.1462
transport	CMF 88	0.0285	0.1665
other	CMF not included elsewhere	0.0367	0.1881
maintenance	CMF 23, 27, 29, 33, 63, 67	0.0592	0.2359
recruiter	Recruiter during 1997–2003 period	0.1051	0.2878

Table 6.2
Data Describing Recruiter Characteristics

Characteristic	Sample Mean
Fraction of recruiters:	
Commanders	0.1508
Term less than one year	0.1584
Term of one to two years	0.2232
Term of two to three years	0.3927
Term three years or above	0.2309
Entering cohort:	
1987	0.1703
1988	0.1596
1989	0.1599
1990	0.1390
1991	0.0852
1992	0.0876
1993	0.0782
1994	0.0434
1995	0.0394
1996	0.0375
Monthly high-quality production	0.8302
Months as recruiter	25.67

period. The next four variables in Table 6.2 reflect the amount of time these soldiers served as recruiters. About 16 percent served for less than a year, more than 20 percent served for a full year but less than two, and almost 40 percent remained in recruiting between 2 and 3 years. Information on average productivity was also gathered; on average these recruiters produced about 0.83 high-quality contracts per month, and about 95 percent of them had monthly write rates of between 0.58 and 1.10.

Enlisted Personnel Career Paths

In this section we estimate logistic models designed to compare recruiters with other enlisted personnel.[3] In Table 6.3, three outcomes are examined. The first model analyzes factors that predict the probability of becoming a recruiter. The next two models examine the probability of being promoted to E-6 and E-7, respectively, by 2003. These models control for a variety of personal characteristics including past promotion rates and cohort year (the 1987 entering cohort is the excluded group).

The first estimated equation shows factors that predict whether a soldier became a recruiter during the 1997–2003 period. Since the recruiting force draws primarily from enlisted personnel near the midpoints of their military service, a person from the 1988 entry cohort was much more likely to become a recruiter by 2003 than someone entering the Army as late as 1996, and as the estimated coefficients of the cohort indicators show, the earlier a soldier entered the more likely it is that that person will have become a recruiter by 2003. There were also significant differences between occupational specialties (maintenance specialties were the omitted category or benchmark for comparison). For example, personnel from combat and transportation specialties were much more likely to become recruiters than were individuals from Army intelligence occupations. Males with no dependents were more likely to be recruiters.

Although enlisted personnel with some college education were slightly less likely to become recruiters, other coefficients strongly suggest that members of the recruiter pool were relatively highly qualified and had successful military careers at the time they became recruiters. For example, soldiers who had relatively high AFQT scores and were high school graduates were more likely to become recruiters. Also revealing is the result that personnel who took longer to be promoted to E-4 and E-5 are significantly less likely to become recruiters.

---

[3]   To test the sensitivity of results to model specification, we also estimated separate regressions for each entering cohort. These are reported in Appendix A, Tables A.6 through A.8. The empirical results and policy implications were largely unaffected by this alternative approach.

Table 6.3
Probability Models of Enlisted Personnel Career Paths

Variable	Probability of Not Becoming Recruiter by 2003		Probability of Not Making E-6 by 2003		Probability of Not Making E-7 by 2003	
Mean:	0.898		0.3718		0.8326	
	Coeff.	Std. Error	Coeff.	Std. Error	Coeff.	Std. Error
Intercept	2.2915	0.2485	−10.5967	0.2057	−7.1382	0.2509
grade4	0.3290	0.0251	1.1257	0.0217	1.0928	0.0261
grade5	0.4326	0.0234	1.7944	0.0213	1.7825	0.0271
depend	0.1895	0.0269	−0.4526	0.0202	−0.0327	0.0294
marry	0.0208	0.0314	−0.2955	0.0250	−0.1606	0.0312
afqt	−0.5780	0.0416	−0.4288	0.0324	−0.5358	0.0427
grad	−0.4265	0.1110	−0.0767	0.0880	−0.2124	0.0948
college	0.0886	0.0448	−0.4350	0.0379	−0.2478	0.0430
white	−0.0869	0.0283	0.1527	0.0212	−0.0661	0.0294
male	−0.4210	0.0484	0.1056	0.0292	0.0499	0.0431
infantry	−0.4728	0.0443	−1.1197	0.0360	−0.4454	0.0457
armor	−0.6319	0.0566	−0.6531	0.0483	−0.2976	0.0622
artillery	−0.6277	0.0476	−0.7539	0.0380	−0.2231	0.0518
signal	−0.4237	0.0577	−0.7004	0.0474	−0.4076	0.0585
admin	−0.0686	0.0618	−0.0182	0.0403	−0.4139	0.0588
technical	−0.0960	0.0667	0.0528	0.0460	0.1603	0.0674
munitions	−0.0883	0.1439	−0.9781	0.1088	−0.4186	0.1407
supply	0.0420	0.0632	0.4935	0.0396	0.0341	0.0615
medical	0.2449	0.0620	0.1300	0.0393	0.2101	0.0577
police	−0.2828	0.0727	−0.4658	0.0542	0.1763	0.0834
food	−0.0999	0.0953	−0.0273	0.0654	−0.2541	0.0835
intel	0.4519	0.0936	−1.0294	0.0693	−0.2020	0.0798
transport	−0.5137	0.0703	0.4480	0.0536	0.4962	0.0823
other	−0.0894	0.0615	−0.5723	0.0460	−0.1702	0.0605
recruiter	—	—	−0.6831	0.0385	−0.2381	0.0345
1988 cohort	0.0409	0.0463	0.4319	0.0643	0.3555	0.0382
1989 cohort	0.1225	0.0468	0.8545	0.0589	0.9172	0.0395
1990 cohort	0.2319	0.0465	1.2143	0.0570	1.4355	0.0414
1991 cohort	0.5404	0.0535	1.6546	0.0582	2.1018	0.0506

Table 6.3—continued

Variable	Probability of Not Becoming Recruiter by 2003		Probability of Not Making E-6 by 2003		Probability of Not Making E-7 by 2003	
Mean:	0.898		0.3718		0.8326	
Variable	Coeff.	Std. Error	Coeff.	Std. Error	Coeff.	Std. Error
1992 cohort	0.7688	0.0525	2.1579	0.0553	2.9498	0.0566
1993 cohort	0.8222	0.0531	2.6313	0.0559	3.9223	0.0740
1994 cohort	1.1975	0.0585	3.2336	0.0565	5.4357	0.1317
1995 cohort	1.3808	0.0587	3.9383	0.0573	*	*
1996 cohort	1.6613	0.0588	4.9387	0.0585	*	*

*None of the 1995 and 1996 entering cohort had achieved E-7 by 2003.

The last two logistic regressions reported in Table 6.3 examined factors that predict achievement of ranks E-6 and E-7 by 2003. Virtually all of those in the early-entering cohorts had reached E-6, but very few from the 1996 cohort had done so. Over all, only about 17 percent of the sample had achieved the E-7 rank. In comparison with maintenance specialists, soldiers in infantry and military intelligence were more likely, and those in supply or logistics occupations less likely, to make E-6. The promotion patterns by MOS for E-7 were similar.

Personal characteristics are also predictive of promotion patterns. Married soldiers with dependents appeared to advance more rapidly. Individuals with more education and higher AFQT scores also tended to advance more rapidly. Finally, the probability of becoming an E-6 or E-7 by 2003 was significantly higher when promotion time to lower ranks (E-4 and E-5) was more rapid.

Of particular interest are the results on promotion to E-6 and E-7 for those soldiers who became recruiters. Keep in mind that the models control for a variety of factors, including the previous performance or revealed personnel quality before becoming a recruiter.[4] Recruiters were more likely to be promoted to E-6 or E-7 than were other per-

---

[4] These regressions are based on comparisons between individuals who did not separate from the Army by 2003. Out of concern about possible selection biases, we also ran models that excluded recruiters still on production in 2003, because that is an indication that they were very likely not to separate in the near future. The results were virtually identical.

sonnel who are otherwise identical in terms of entry year, past promotion rates, occupational specialty, and various measured personal
characteristics.

Using the logistic regression estimates reported in Table 6.3, some
predicted probabilities are presented in Table 6.4. Comparisons are
made with a baseline prediction, reflecting average or "typical" sample
characteristics. High past performers, defined as individuals who had
experienced rapid advancement to both E-4 and E-5,[5] with otherwise
average characteristics, had higher probabilities of becoming recruiters: 11.7 percent in comparison to 8.1 percent. In contrast, low past
performers only had a 5.6 percent chance of becoming recruiters. In
other words, high performers were more than twice as likely to join the
recruiting force. Moreover, those with some college and AFQT scores
in category II or higher were twice as likely to become recruiters than
non–high school graduates with lower AFQT scores. Clearly, recruiters
are a select group.

Table 6.4 also provides probability estimates for promotion to
E-6. The benchmark prediction for a typical enlisted nonrecruiter is 71.6
percent. In contrast, predictions for plus or minus one deviation from

Table 6.4
Model Simulations: Enlisted Personnel Career Paths

	Prob (recruiter)	Prob (E-6)
Sample means	0.081	0.716
High performers (time to E-4, E-5)	0.117	0.925
Low performers (time to E-4, E-5)	0.056	0.353
Low AFQT, nongrad	0.045	0.669
High AFQT, college	0.090	0.812
Infantry	0.102	0.837
Intel	0.043	0.824
Maintenance	0.066	0.625

---

[5] Rapid advancement is defined as one standard deviation below the sample mean for both
of the variables grade4 and grade5, which are defined as the logarithms of the number of
months of service before being promoted to E-4 and E-5, respectively.

the sample average in past promotion speed range from 35.3 percent to 92.5 percent for low and high performers, respectively. Individuals with low AFQT scores and no high school diploma had only a 66.9 percent chance of making it to E-6 by 2003, while soldiers with relatively high test scores and some college had an 81.2 percent probability.

Table 6.5 presents average effects of serving as a recruiter on promotion for each entry cohort. These simulations are for all recruiters, regardless of their productivity, tenure, or job responsibilities. A nonrecruiter who joined the Army in 1988 had a 93.4 percent probability of becoming an E-6 and a 38.8 percent probability of becoming an E-7 by 2003 (if that soldier remained in the Army until 2003). For those who served as recruiters, the corresponding probabilities of achieving E-6 or E-7 were higher, at 96.6 percent and 44.5 percent, respectively. The same pattern exists for the later cohorts, albeit with the probabilities of promotion being lower for later-entering cohorts. For example, for the cohort that entered in 1996, only 13.5 percent of the non-recruiters had achieved the E-6 rank by 2003, while for recruiters, this probability (holding many other factors constant) was almost twice as high, at 23.6 percent.

Table 6.5
Average Recruiter Effects on Promotion, by Entry Cohort

Cohort (entered in year)	Probability of Reaching E-6		Probability of Reaching E-7	
	Recruiter	Nonrecruiter	Recruiter	Nonrecruiter
1988	0.966	0.934	0.445	0.388
1989	0.948	0.903	0.314	0.265
1990	0.928	0.866	0.214	0.177
1991	0.892	0.806	0.123	0.099
1992	0.833	0.716	0.057	0.045
1993	0.756	0.611	0.022	0.018
1994	0.630	0.462	0.005	0.004
1995	0.457	0.298	0.000	0.000
1996	0.236	0.135	0.000	0.000

Implications for Recruiter Selection

Using the recruiting productivity differences associated with observable individual characteristics (see Chapter Two), one can assess whether the Army is selecting for recruiting the personnel who would be most productive as recruiters. From a cost-benefit perspective, however, assignments should not be made solely on the basis of predicted recruiting success. For example, there are equity and political constraints. In addition, the Army may not wish to assign to recruiting personnel in occupations of critical need, significant training investments, or high levels of job satisfaction. For example, the analysis of productivity presented in Table 2.2 indicates that individuals in Army intelligence fields are, on average, better recruiters than those from other occupations. However, these individuals are less likely to become recruiters (Table 6.3). From a cost-benefit perspective, this is probably sound policy.

Still, systematic differences in productivity should be given considerable weight in the assignment process. To see whether this was the case, we also examined whether selection characteristics could be linked to a measure of recruiter success other than contract production, which was examined in Table 2.2. This alternative measure, which is based on tenure as a recruiter, abstracts from different recruiting conditions faced by different recruiters, and therefore might more accurately represent success relative to a peer group.[6] Table 6.6 documents logistic models that examine the probability of remaining as a recruiter for more than one year as well as the probability of serving three or fewer years. In general, longer tenures are indicative of a good match between the individual and recruiting. Table 6.7 presents simulations, using estimates in Table 6.6 for recruiters who had slow, average, and fast promotions to E-4 and E-5 before becoming recruiters. Clearly, those who had early career success were more likely to continue as a

---

[6] As we will see below, the average productivity of a recruiter over his or her term of service is highly affected by the period of time during which the soldier was a recruiter. Mission levels fluctuated dramatically over the 1997–2003 period, as did economic conditions. Since our sample mixes personnel who served during different periods, their average level of production may not reflect how well they performed relative to their peers during the same period.

Table 6.6
Probability of Recruiter Tenure

Variable	Tenure Less Than 1 Year		Tenure More Than 3 Years	
	Coefficient	Standard Error	Coefficient	Standard Error
Intercept	2.1674	0.8623	2.4081	1.4046
grade4	−0.1394	0.0900	0.2740	0.1010
grade5	−0.3471	0.0899	0.3130	0.0995
depend	−0.3702	0.0962	0.6836	0.0985
marry	0.1377	0.1095	−0.1003	0.1179
afqt	−0.2514	0.1508	0.3301	0.1631
grad	0.5288	0.3099	−0.5225	0.4445
college	−0.0221	0.1526	0.0234	0.1717
white	−0.2624	0.0998	0.0564	0.1105
male	0.2983	0.1562	−0.2517	0.1941
infantry	0.1921	0.1540	−0.6861	0.1784
armor	−0.1663	0.1906	−0.0841	0.2459
artillery	0.2240	0.1707	−0.4716	0.1936
signal	−0.0352	0.1928	−0.1972	0.2413
admin	−0.1292	0.2111	−0.1420	0.2642
technical	0.1219	0.2536	−0.2420	0.2861
munitions	0.7019	0.5559	−0.1061	0.5648
supply	−0.0514	0.2218	−0.0456	0.2770
medical	0.0363	0.2150	−0.3867	0.2421
police	0.1726	0.2560	−0.4775	0.2892
food	0.3580	0.3543	−0.0171	0.3789
intel	−0.5500	0.2831	0.4284	0.4628
transport	−0.1404	0.2421	−0.6294	0.2764
other	−0.2036	0.1974	−0.3510	0.2426
1987 cohort	1.2895	0.2151	−3.5091	1.0126
1988 cohort	1.6032	0.2205	−3.6995	1.0122
1989 cohort	1.7209	0.2234	−3.5929	1.0130
1990 cohort	1.4518	0.2200	−3.4602	1.0133
1991 cohort	1.5647	0.2403	−3.5566	1.0176
1992 cohort	1.8927	0.2497	−3.4661	1.0172
1993 cohort	1.0973	0.2322	−3.3180	1.0199
1994 cohort	0.7579	0.2559	−1.7311	1.0892
1995 cohort	0.4082	0.2530	0.0741	1.4211

Table 6.7
Impact of Past Promotion Speed on Recruiter Tenure

Time to E-4, E-5	Prob (Tenure < 1 year)	Prob (Tenure = 3+ years)
Slow*	0.2645	0.1193
Average	0.2170	0.1560
Fast**	0.1760	0.2014

*One standard deviation above mean of both log(time to E-4) and log(time to E-5).

**One standard deviation below mean of both log(time to E-4) and log(time to E-5).

recruiter for at least a year and twice as likely as those with slow promotions to remain in recruiting for a long period.

Table 6.8 summarizes findings about effects of selected individual characteristics on recruiter selection and measures of performance.[7] A plus, minus, or zero indicates that the characteristic had a positive, negative, or no effect, respectively, on the outcome measure. The symbol "NA" means that the role of the characteristic could not be analyzed for that outcome. Note that a soldier is more likely to become a recruiter if that soldier: has a relatively high AFQT score; is a high school graduate, male, or over 35 years of age; has a combat MOS; or was promoted to E-4 and E-5 relatively rapidly. Of these factors, several are also associated with being successful in the Army generally, as measured by the probability of promotion to E-6, as well as being successful recruiters. For example, individuals from combat specialties (including infantry, armor, and artillery) are more likely to be assigned to recruiting, are promoted faster to E-6, spend more time as recruiters, and write more contracts per month. Nonetheless, these results are not sufficient to conclude that more recruiters should come from combat arms occupations, because such soldiers appear to be highly valued in the mainstream Army as revealed by their relatively rapid promotion rates.

---

[7] The summary results for the probability of becoming a recruiter and the probability of being promoted to E-6 are from Table 6.3. The results for recruiter tenure are from Table 6.6. The last column summarizes results on individual recruiter productivity reported in Table 2.2.

Table 6.8
Personnel Attributes: Effects on Recruiter Selection and Performance

	Prob(Rec)	Prob(E-6)	Recruiter Tenure < 1	Recruiter Productivity
High AFQT	+	+	−	0
High school grad	+	0	+	0
College	−	+	0	0
Single	0	−	0	0
Dependents	−	+	−	+
Male	+	0	+	+
Age < 30	−	NA	NA	+
Age > 35	+	NA	NA	−
Technical MOS	0	0	0	+
Intel MOS	−	+	−	+
Combat MOS	+	+	+	+
Past performance	+	+	+	NA

In contrast, soldiers older than 35 are more likely to become recruiters, although the evidence indicates that younger recruiters are more productive. This suggests that the Army should consider assigning more young personnel, such as corporals, to serve as recruiters.

For those with at least some college, the probability of being assigned to recruiting is lower. This makes sense, since those individuals succeed in general, but there is no evidence that they make better recruiters. Individuals with high AFQT scores are more likely to be selected as recruiters. However, although they are generally successful in the Army, their recruiting productivity is no higher and they are less likely to last a full year in recruiting. Individuals with dependents are less likely to be assigned, and they appear to be productive in the mainstream Army as well as in recruiting. However, their expected tenure is lower, and as a result they may not be desirable candidates for assignment.[8] Finally, soldiers from Army intelligence are less likely to be assigned to recruiting, even though the evidence suggests that they

---

[8] The available data did not enable us to distinguish between recruiters who volunteered and those who were assigned. Some of the observed relationships could well be dependent on this distinction.

are more productive as recruiters. However, given the high opportunity cost of assigning these soldiers to recruiting (i.e., the lost value of their work in intelligence) and in view of their relatively short tenure as recruiters, the assignment process appears to be working well.

Rewarding Recruiter Productivity

We have seen that the recruiter assignment process tends to select relatively good performers and does not appear to reduce their promotion prospects. If anything, future advancement is more rapid than otherwise anticipated, even when one controls for revealed ability and a large number of observable characteristics.[9] However, an important question remains. Does the career path depend on whether the recruiter is successful in recruiting?

To answer this question, we considered several measures of recruiting success and how they relate to the probabilities of promotion to E-6 and E-7. First, we considered length of tenure in recruiting. We also considered individual and station productivity both in absolute and relative terms. To foreshadow our results, what we found was striking. In particular, recruiters appear to be highly rewarded for their productivity relative to others who recruited during the same time period, rather than for their absolute productivity levels.[10] Moreover, although rewards for being productive in recruiting are substantial, there appear to be few penalties for failure.

In Table 6.9, results of logistic regression analyses of achieving E-6 and E-7 are reported for the full sample of enlisted personnel. Recall

---

[9]   Two caveats are in order. Recruiter data were available only for the later portion of the time period analyzed. Although many of the personnel examined had returned to other RA occupations by 2003, our promotion snapshot occurred only a short time after completion of the recruiting tour. Thus, it remains possible that deleterious ramifications of recruiting duty were experienced several years after their return to their primary occupations. In addition, it is possible that such effects differ by occupation. These issues should be examined in future research.

[10]   Doing so may be very advantageous because evaluating performance relative to other recruiters during the same time periods may control to a large degree for the national-level fluctuations in recruiting difficulty.

that these models control for numerous factors, including entry cohort and revealed ability as indicated by previous promotion rates. However, instead of a single recruiter indicator variable, the model included four separate variables reflecting the length of recruiting service. Recruiters serving less than one year did not appear to be any more or less likely to be promoted to E-6 or E-7 than other enlisted personnel. (The coefficient estimates were not statistically significant for the shortest tenure.) But recruiters with longer tenures in recruiting were more likely to be promoted than nonrecruiters, and the positive effect of recruiting was highest for those recruiters who spent at least three years in recruiting.

Simulations illustrating the relationships between recruiter tenure and the likelihood of promotion to E-6 and E-7 are presented in Table 6.10. In comparison with a soldier who was never a recruiter, a recruiter with a long term of duty was substantially more likely to have achieved at least E-6 by 2003 (94 percent versus 72 percent). The impact on the probability of achieving E-7 was also pronounced; for nonrecruiters, the chances were less than 1 in 20 (4.6 percent), but for recruiters serving three or more years, the probability was almost four times as high (17.6 percent).

We also considered, for recruiters only, alternatively replacing recruiting tenure with two more direct measures of recruiting success in regressions analogous to those reported in Table 6.9. These measures were (1) the individual's average monthly productivity or write rate (high-quality contracts per month), and (2) the average station production ratio (the recruiter's home station's contracts divided by the mission). The estimates suggested a negative, but statistically insignificant, association between promotion and these two absolute measures of achievement.

These anomalous results stemmed from two factors. First, the observed level of production was highly dependent on the time period during which the recruiter served. This was important because, as illustrated in Appendix A, Table A.9, there were significant differences in the typical performance of recruiters within the 1997–2003 time period. For example, the average production ratio for stations was under 0.50

Table 6.9
Impact of Recruiter Tenure on Promotion Probabilities,
All Enlisted Personnel

Variable	Probability of Not Making E-6		Probability of Not Making E-7	
	Estimate	Standard Error	Estimate	Standard Error
Intercept	−10.5928	0.2097	−3.6887	0.2305
grade4	1.1468	0.0222	0.9869	0.0257
grade5	1.7941	0.0216	1.1760	0.0235
depend	−0.4557	0.0207	−0.3399	0.0272
marry	−0.2873	0.0255	−0.3319	0.0286
afqt	−0.4507	0.0330	−0.2168	0.0392
grad	−0.0602	0.0892	0.2072	0.0901
college	−0.4249	0.0386	−0.4187	0.0384
white	0.1475	0.0217	−0.0878	0.0269
male	0.1056	0.0296	−0.1179	0.0393
infantry	−1.1294	0.0368	−0.5410	0.0422
armor	−0.6636	0.0496	−0.1482	0.0581
artillery	−0.7393	0.0388	−0.2110	0.0482
signal	−0.6972	0.0483	−0.3877	0.0554
admin	−0.0335	0.0410	−0.4530	0.0542
technical	0.0408	0.0470	0.0147	0.0638
munitions	−0.9561	0.1102	−0.4710	0.1228
supply	0.4887	0.0403	0.0060	0.0575
medical	0.1375	0.0398	−0.0571	0.0542
police	−0.4668	0.0554	0.1752	0.0762
food	−0.0117	0.0662	−0.6482	0.0803
intel	−1.0396	0.0703	−0.3445	0.0697
transport	0.4232	0.0550	0.4261	0.0815
other	−0.5798	0.0469	−0.2441	0.0551
1988 cohort	0.4463	0.0658	−1.7736	0.0353
1989 cohort	0.8648	0.0603	−1.2443	0.0364
1990 cohort	1.2228	0.0585	−0.7505	0.0382
1991 cohort	1.6595	0.0596	−0.1833	0.0470
1992 cohort	2.1691	0.0567	0.6472	0.0536

Table 6.9—continued

Variable	Probability of Not Making E-6		Probability of Not Making E-7	
	Estimate	Standard Error	Estimate	Standard Error
1993 cohort	2.6354	0.0573	1.5053	0.0719
1994 cohort	3.2377	0.0579	2.8812	0.1318
1995 cohort	3.9339	0.0587	-	-
1996 cohort	4.9304	0.0600	-	-
Recruiter, term of service:				
Term < 1 year	0.0385	0.1021	−0.1667	0.1004
Term 1 to 2 years	−0.8336	0.1254	−0.5643	0.0899
Term 2 to 3 years	−0.8972	0.0998	−0.5636	0.0672
Term 3 or more years	−1.6506	0.2345	−1.8689	0.0980

Table 6.10
Recruiter Tenure and Predicted Promotion Probabilities

Recruiter Tenure	Prob (E-6)	Prob (E-7)
Never a recruiter	0.7240	0.0460
Recruiter, term of service		
Term < 1 year	0.7504	0.0374
Term 1 to 2 years	0.8779	0.0546
Term 2 to 3 years	0.8846	0.0546
Term 3 or more years	0.9421	0.1757

in 1998, but it was over 1.0 in 2002. If performance were evaluated in relative rather than absolute terms, then a station achieving a ratio of 0.75 would be viewed as successful in 1998, but unsuccessful four years later.

The relationship between promotion and productivity in recruiting was further complicated by the fact that recruiters who are relatively unsuccessful are more likely to leave the recruiting force. To illustrate the possible selection bias, imagine two recruiters who started recruiting during the last quarter of 1997, when average station production ratios were about 0.8. Assume that one recruiter has average success, with a ratio of 0.8, and that the other recruiter was rather unproductive, with a ratio of 0.6. Assume further that the former was retained for another year, but the latter was asked to leave the recruiting force with a career production ratio of 0.6. However, the successful recruiter faced poor recruiting conditions in 1998, when the average production ratio was considerably lower at 0.4. The retained recruiter, after a 12-month period of average productivity, then may have had a career average of about 0.5. Thus, the better recruiter, because he or she was retained during bad times, actually had a lower average productivity than the relatively poor recruiter who was forced to leave when times were good.

Thus, absolute performance measures—that is, measures that don't compare results to those of others recruiting during the same time period—do not appear to be attractive for evaluation and promotion purposes. To take account of the time periods of recruiting service, relative performance measures were computed based on the years of entry and exit from the recruiting force using results of regressions reported in Appendix A, Table A.10.[11] Actual station ratios were then divided by predicted or average station ratios to form an index of relative station performance. This index was scaled to average 1.000 (for average relative performance) and has a standard deviation of 0.355.

Table 6.11 presents predicted probabilities of various career outcomes for various values of the station relative performance index, based on regressions reported in Appendix A, Table A.11. (The five values of the index are its mean plus and minus one and two standard deviations.) These results reveal strong relationships between the index and both recruiting tenure and rates of separation from the Army by 2003. More specifically, recruiters in relatively productive stations are much more likely to remain in recruiting and much less likely to leave the Army altogether.

---

[11] Station performance for each recruiter was regressed on a series of dummy variables representing all of the recruiting-year/tenure combinations in the sample. The recruiting year for this sample was defined as the first year the individual became a recruiter. Tenure is based on the length of service as a recruiter. The predictions can be interpreted as the average production ratio of recruiting stations over the same period of service.

Table 6.11
Relative Station Performance and Career Outcomes: Simulations

	Prob (tenure < 1)	Prob (tenure < 2)	Prob (tenure < 3)	Prob (leaving Army by 2003)
Station performance				
0.290	0.3725	0.6113	0.8884	0.2148
0.645	0.2865	0.5620	0.8480	0.1710
1.000	0.2136	0.5114	0.7963	0.1346
1.355	0.1552	0.4606	0.7327	0.1050
1.710	0.1105	0.4106	0.6577	0.0812

The estimated effects of relative station performance on promotion probabilities are reported in the last row of Table 6.12. Probabilities of advancement to E-6 and E-7 are significantly higher the higher is the station's performance. Table 6.13 simulates the impacts for different performance ratios. A recruiter in an average station (index = 1.000) would have a probability of about 83.3 percent of reaching E-6 by 2003. The range of predicted probabilities for recruiters in low- to high-performing stations was 0.78 to 0.87. Moreover, promotion to E-7 could be more than twice as likely depending on how productive the recruiter's station was in relative terms.

Finally, Table 6.14 examines one more measure of performance, namely the probability that a soldier would leave the Army between 2001 and 2003.[12] As in the previous logistic regressions, controls for a variety of factors were included. Simulations based on this regression are reported in Table 6.15. For example, soldiers with high AFQT scores and fast promotion rates to E-4 and E-5 were more likely to separate. In contrast, individuals serving as recruiters were less likely to leave the Army.

---

[12] In these analyses, we used a sample of roughly 140,000 individuals who were still in active service in 2000. We also included only those recruiters who had completed their term of service as recruiters by 2003. Since we wished to examine the impact of the recruiting experience on retention, we needed to include individuals who had actually left the Army by the end of the 2003 period. In addition, because our recruiter service data begins in 1997, we wished to examine a period beginning at least three years later, namely 2000, because individuals planning to retire in the near future are unlikely to be assigned to recruiting.

Table 6.12
Probability of Recruiter Promotion: Effect of Station Performance

Variable	Probability Not Promoted to E-6		Probability Not Promoted to E-7	
	Coefficient	Standard Error	Coefficient	Standard Error
Intercept	−7.2495	0.9794	−6.0234	0.8251
grade4	0.6724	0.1034	0.7286	0.0863
grade5	1.0088	0.1044	1.3401	0.0906
depend	−0.3711	0.0984	0.2003	0.0901
marry	−0.5161	0.1336	−0.3698	0.0994
afqt	−0.0691	0.1691	−0.1448	0.1393
grad	−0.4364	0.3780	−0.0934	0.3137
college	−0.5074	0.1891	−0.3592	0.1426
white	0.3938	0.1123	0.1639	0.0944
male	0.0165	0.1649	0.1800	0.1512
infantry	−0.7486	0.1699	0.3240	0.1462
armor	−0.2603	0.2181	0.3618	0.1931
artillery	−0.8145	0.2023	0.0387	0.1555
signal	−0.3963	0.2211	−0.1864	0.1827
admin	0.5724	0.2083	−0.1717	0.2048
technical	0.2327	0.2478	0.6360	0.2590
munitions	−0.7908	0.5358	−0.9235	0.4174
supply	0.5349	0.2258	−0.0637	0.2092
medical	−0.0824	0.2374	−0.1353	0.1922
police	−0.0825	0.2580	0.4920	0.2623
food	0.0262	0.3294	−0.1408	0.2756
intel	−0.5878	0.3402	0.1898	0.3014
transport	−0.0650	0.2711	0.4658	0.2450
other	0.0447	0.2136	0.1402	0.1972

Table 6.12—continued

Variable	Probability Not Promoted to E-6		Probability Not Promoted to E-7	
	Coefficient	Standard Error	Coefficient	Standard Error
1988 cohort	0.3149	0.2381	0.1944	0.1179
1989 cohort	0.8121	0.2227	0.8352	0.1256
1990 cohort	1.1763	0.2196	1.2285	0.1337
1991 cohort	1.2806	0.2369	1.4580	0.1626
1992 cohort	1.9197	0.2218	2.4217	0.1912
1993 cohort	2.3536	0.2259	3.1007	0.2503
1994 cohort	2.7375	0.2543	4.3126	0.5204
1995 cohort	3.6140	0.2599		
1996 cohort	4.2045	0.2745		
Station performance	−0.4680	0.1546	−0.6089	0.1260

Table 6.13
Station Performance and Promotion Probabilities: Simulations

Station Performance	Prob (E-6)	Prob (E-7)
0.290	0.7816	0.0377
0.645	0.8086	0.0464
1.000	0.8330	0.0570
1.355	0.8549	0.0698
1.710	0.8743	0.0852

Table 6.14
Probability of Not Separating, 2001–2003

	Coefficient	Standard Error
Intercept	2.1591	0.1872
grade4	0.1623	0.0201
grade5	0.3561	0.0179
depend	0.1877	0.0192
marry	0.0064	0.0235
afqt	−0.5063	0.0314
grad	0.1220	0.0791
college	−0.0107	0.0315
white	−0.2864	0.0207
male	0.2375	0.0271
infantry	0.0909	0.0329
artillery	0.2213	0.0384
signal	−0.1173	0.0423
admin	0.0961	0.0402
technical	0.1217	0.0464
munitions	0.0631	0.1009
supply	0.0283	0.0396
other	0.1032	0.0434
1988 cohort	−0.2249	0.0553
1989 cohort	−0.6260	0.0509
1990 cohort	−0.7529	0.0495
1991 cohort	−0.8235	0.0509
1992 cohort	−0.8617	0.0484
1993 cohort	−0.8975	0.0483
1994 cohort	−0.9405	0.0482
1995 cohort	−0.9163	0.0477
1996 cohort	0.1834	0.0482
recruiter	0.5662	0.0488

Table 6.15
Predicted Probability of Separation, 2001–2003

Baseline (average)	0.1780
Black male	0.1137
High AFQT*	0.2043
Fast promotion time*	0.2221
Recruiter	0.1095

*One standard deviation above sample average for promotion to both E-4 and E-5.

CHAPTER SEVEN

Implications for Effective Recruiter Management

In this chapter we discuss implications of our analyses for improving recruiter management. In particular, we consider implications of our findings for human resource policies in the areas of selecting soldiers for recruiting duty, assigning recruiters to stations, missioning to promote equity across recruiters, missioning to increase recruiting production, using promotions to motivate and reward recruiters, and screening out recruiters who are underproducing.

Costs and Benefits of Resource Management Policies: Overview

In general, our research demonstrates that various types of human resource management policies can be very helpful in meeting the Army's recruiting requirements. For example, we have found that several types of policies can have important effects on the flow of high-quality enlistments. Although the gains from individual policy changes appear to be modest, implementing several policies in combination could save the Army hundreds of millions of dollars annually. Indeed, each 1 percent increase in high-quality enlistments generated by a more effective management approach can save the Army $3.6 million in recruiter costs on an annual basis.[1]

---

[1] Using the recruiter elasticity estimates described in Chapter Four, we computed that the marginal cost of one additional high-quality recruit would be approximately $6,000. Thus, a 1 percent increase in high-quality enlistments, which would be about 600 additional recruits

Actions that provide such savings in recruiting costs, however, can conflict with the attainment of other Army goals both within USAREC and elsewhere. In addition, many of the potential effects on other Army goals are very hard to quantify. Consider three examples. First, assigning unusually good soldiers to recruiting involves relatively high burdens on the commands losing some of their most highly valued personnel. Second, a reallocation of missions that promotes efficiency (i.e., increases recruiter productivity) may be viewed as unfair if it calls for significant increases in effort by only some recruiters. Finally, although higher promotion rates for successful recruiters appear desirable in terms of increasing aggregate recruiter productivity, this policy could diminish the morale of soldiers not selected for recruiting or who end up being relatively unproductive recruiters merely because they were assigned to especially difficult markets, were unlucky during their tours of duty, or both. Thus, our empirical analyses, which focus on policies aimed at increasing aggregate recruiter productivity and promoting equity among recruiters, do not address other impacts on the Army, especially impacts outside of the Recruiting Command.

Recruiter Selection

The analyses reported in Chapter Two provide several new insights about characteristics of productive recruiters. These insights can help improve decisions about which soldiers to select for recruiting duty.

- **Some recruiter characteristics are very helpful in predicting recruiter productivity.**

The recruiter attributes included in our econometric models in Chapter Two were very helpful in explaining across-recruiter differences in contract production. In combination, attributes such as recruiter gender, age, AFQT, race, education, and occupational specialty account for about 7.5 percent of differences in individual produc-

---

per year, would cost about $3.6 million. Of course, the savings would be much greater if the Army relied on salary increases to generate new enlistments.

tivity (Table 2.6). In fact, recruiters' personal attributes are almost as important as missions or local economic conditions and demographics in explaining variation in production levels. In addition, other persistent but unobserved characteristics (at least in the data available to us) of recruiters (e.g., personality, energy, talent for selling) account for very large productivity differences that are significantly higher than those associated with the individual attributes we could measure and include in our models (Table 2.7). Substantial emphasis should be placed on developing methods for identifying those personal attributes that are most predictive of productivity in recruiting.[2]

- **Young recruiters are more productive.**

Our results indicate that recruiters under the age of 30 are significantly more productive than older recruiters, including career recruiters (Table 2.2). By adding about 500 young recruiters and reducing the number of older recruiters (over 35) by the same number, the Army could increase overall productivity by about 1 percent. If the opportunity cost of reassigning younger soldiers is lower than that for more senior personnel, it makes sense for the Army to consider a younger recruiting force. Another issue to be considered, however, is the MOS-specific effects of interrupting younger soldiers' careers for temporary assignment to recruiting.

- **Recruiters from traditional military occupations are more productive.**

Recruiters who have been trained in "military" jobs, such as combat arms or intelligence, make more productive recruiters than those from jobs more likely to be found in the private sector, such as maintenance or logistics (Table 2.2). As discussed above, the productivity of soldiers as recruiters is but one-half of the cost-benefit calculation. For example,

---

[2] We are aware of ongoing Army research efforts to develop better methods for predicting recruiter effectiveness *ex ante*. When they become available, measures used to select soldiers for recruiting duty should be incorporated into empirical analyses of recruiting outcomes (such as the ones in Chapters Two, Three, and Four) so that their impacts on productivity in the field can be assessed.

the opportunity cost of assigning a soldier to recruiting can be very high if the soldier has skills that are of high priority, in short supply, or involve unusually high training costs.

- **Empirical results suggest one potential problem with private contracting.**

The fact that younger personnel, who have more recently been employed in traditional military specialties, are more productive as recruiters indicates that contract or civilian recruiters may not be as effective, all things equal. Contractors are likely to be older, retired military personnel whom young prospects are less likely to trust or relate to as role models.

Recruiter Assignment

The results in Chapter Two also provide several new insights about how the attributes of recruiters and their local markets interact to affect recruiter productivity. These results can help improve decisions about assignment of recruiters to individual stations.

- **Recruiters who are similar to the population in their stations' territories are more successful.**

As we have seen, younger recruiters are more effective than older ones. There is other evidence that potential enlistees identify more with recruiters with similar characteristics. For example, we found that female recruiters sign more women than do men, but they are less successful in recruiting men (Tables 2.2, A.3). African American recruiters are up to 4 percent more productive than non-Hispanic, white recruiters in signing high-quality prospects in markets with large black populations (Table 2.4). Although equity considerations make it impossible to select and assign recruiters based solely on gender or race, there is a large payoff to both the recruiter and the Army in getting the right recruiters to markets in which they are most likely to be productive.[3]

• **Recruiters assigned to their home states are more productive.**

Recruiters who return to the state where they enlisted are also more likely to have things in common with the local population. In the 2001–2003 time period, about 27 percent of all recruiters were located in their home state (Table 2.1). These recruiters are about 3.3 percent more productive, all other things equal. Although it is likely to be infeasible to assign all recruiters to their home states, doubling the number would yield almost 1 percent more high-quality contracts overall. Increasing the number is worth considering.[4] One attractive option, given the results on young recruiters, would be to expand programs that enable recent enlistees to help with recruiting at their home-area stations.

---

[3] In large part the Army is able to accomplish this, probably through USAREC's attempts to assign recruiters to a battalion within the sets they most prefer and battalion and company decisions to assign recruiters to specific stations. For example, although the percentage of African American recruiters is 33 percent in the sample, only 17 percent of recruiters in predominantly white markets are black. In contrast, African Americans represent about 75 percent of the recruiters in markets where the population is at least 50 percent African American.

[4] We realize that USAREC is constrained in attempting to assign a new recruiter to battalions with vacancies in stations where he or she would fit the market especially well (and are high on the recruiter's list of preferred battalions). In particular, in any month USAREC has a set of new recruiters, with specific attributes, to assign, and a key criterion in the assignment is increasing the numbers of recruiters assigned to battalions with the largest proportions of vacancies (i.e., battalions that have relatively low ratios of recruiters assigned to recruiters authorized or "faces to spaces"). However, our results may indicate that the value of making particularly good matches between spaces and faces is higher than previously believed. If so, USAREC, battalions, and companies might consider innovative approaches to improving this matching. For example, it may be worthwhile to assign recruiters to especially appropriate stations a month or two before an opening is expected to occur or delaying assignment of some new recruiters for a month or two until an especially appropriate slot opens up.

Setting Missions to Achieve Equity

The Army has two primary concerns in setting performance goals for stations, namely, increasing enlistments of high-quality youth and treating recruiters fairly. Our analyses provide new insights relevant to both concerns. In this section we discuss implications of our analyses in Chapter Three related to how missions might be adjusted to equalize across stations their chances to achieve their regular Army recruiting goals.

- **Month-to-month variation in performance targets is the key factor in predicting success.**

Success or failure in a particular month is substantially affected by that month's performance goals, namely, missions plus DEP losses for senior alphas (I-IIIA), grad alphas (I-IIIA), and others. For example, adding a single senior alpha mission to a station's performance target has three times the negative impact on the probability of meeting the station's regular Army goals as a halving of the local unemployment rate (Table 3.3).

- **The awards incentive system may underreward production of high-quality contracts.**

Model estimates indicate that senior and graduate I-IIIA prospects are about three times as difficult to recruit as lower-quality youth (Table 3.3). At the same time, the Army reward system provides points in a two-to-one ratio for high- versus lower-quality contracts and awards mission box bonus points to any recruiter signing at least one contract as long as the station makes mission. This may induce recruiters to direct too much effort to lower-quality prospects at the expense of the more desirable senior and grad alphas.

- **Significant inequities exist from market to market and from month to month.**

The current missioning process results in substantial variation in the probabilities of success across stations and over months (Tables 3.2, 3.5, 3.6). Such variation in mission difficulty can be lessened through more careful consideration of demographic factors such as veteran populations and local economic conditions in assigning missions. On average, minority and low-income markets have missions that are too challenging (Table 3.7). In addition, high-quality missions are not adequately adjusted to take into account other demands on recruiting station resources, including reserve and "other" regular Army mission targets (Tables 3.7, 3.8).

- **From an equity perspective, the current treatment of stations with USAR recruiters is problematic.**

Our econometric analyses indicate that, on average, a reserve-recruiting requirement does not affect the probability of a station achieving its regular Army mission box (Table 3.3). This seems to be due to a rough balancing of two opposing forces. On the one hand, increases in reserve recruiters, holding reserve missions constant, aid regular Army recruiting, indicating the presence of positive spillovers or joint-production efficiencies (Tables 3.2, 3.5). On the other hand, increasing the USAR mission, holding constant the size of the USAR recruiting force, undermines regular Army recruiting performance, indicating competition between regular Army and USAR recruiters for some candidates (Tables 3.2, 3.5). Variations in these factors cause significant variation across stations from month to month. In fact, variation in the USAR mission has roughly as much significance as market demographics or the local economy (Table 3.4).

Most starkly, the average probability of a station with reserve recruiters making both its USAR and regular Army mission box is less than half the probability of a station without reserve recruiters making its regular Army mission (Table 3.9). This creates a significant inequity. Regular Army and USAR missions are determined independently, but coordination could promote both equity and efficiency.

Setting Missions to Increase Production

In this section we discuss implications of our analyses in Chapters Four and Five related to how missions might have been adjusted to increase the numbers of high-quality enlistments during our sample period.

- **Performance goals are a key determinant of recruiter effort and production.**

    Variations in missions and DEP losses, taken together, are as important as all other factors in explaining variations in productivity across station months (Table 4.2). The evidence indicates that recruiters work harder in response to higher missions and that extra effort increases production (Table 4.1). We found no evidence that recruiters in any station became so discouraged by the difficulty of their performance goals that they reduced effort in response to greater challenges, given the range of circumstances prevailing from January 2001 through June 2003.

- **Production of high-quality enlistments could be increased by increasing missions, but there are limits and pitfalls.**

    Our estimates indicate that increasing high-quality missions would have induced greater effort, and our simulations (Policy VIII in Chapter Five) indicate that during the period covered by our observations, a 15 percent increase in total missions, if assigned to the half of stations that would be most responsive, could have increased high-quality enlistments by over 7 percent relative to the status quo (Table 5.1). Such an opportunity could be well worth exploiting, but there are some caveats to keep in mind. First, the marginal impacts of increasing missions diminish as the missions become more difficult. So, for example, increasing the missions by 30 percent by doubling the scale of Policy VIII would lead to much less than a 14 percent increase in enlistments. Second, the increased productivity may come at a long-run cost because only a fraction of the extra contracts missioned would actually be attained, and effort levels are estimated to be higher for stations with higher recent ratios of production to mission (Table 4.1). Thus, very challenging missions may induce extraordinary levels of effort in the short run, but decrease production ratios and, as a result, reduce morale and opportunities to induce more effort in the longer run. In short, unrealistic missions can create an atmosphere of failure and low morale, and, as a result, reduce future effort and productivity. Finally, the difficulty of recruiting has changed dramatically since 2003. As a result, higher missions may be unachievable today; if so, raising them could prove counterproductive

- **To increase high-quality production, mission allocations should reflect market quality and recruiter response.**

Since recruiters respond to performance goals, but the degree of response varies significantly from market to market, the mission allocation process can significantly affect recruiting outcomes. Econometric analysis of existing data that could be matched to station areas provides guidance about how mission allocations might be improved. Productivity increases of up to 2.7 percent (Table 5.1, Policy III) could have been achieved by reallocating missions across stations and months. Such productivity improvements, achieved by reallocating a fixed total mission, could be almost costless.

Productivity improvements achieved by adopting a mission allocation scheme based on our econometric model could save significant resources. For example, imagine that the Army needed to increase annual high-quality contracts by 10,000, or about 15 percent. Our estimates indicate that increasing mission by 10,000 across the board (Table 5.1, Policy VII) would have yielded 3,420 additional enlistments, resulting in a shortfall of 6,580. To make mission, the Army might expend other resources, such as increases in pay or enlistment bonuses. Using the marginal cost estimate of $6,000 per recruit through recruiter increases, this would cost nearly $40 million. On the other hand, by selectively increasing missions for the highest-impact stations (Table 5.1, Policy VIII), high-quality contracts would increase by 4,440 (rather than 3,420), even without additional resources. To make up the difference, pay increases would total $33 million, saving $7 million in relation to the across-the-board mission increase.

- **Efficient missioning requires reliance on past performance.**

Only about 20 percent of the simulated gains to mission realloca-tions (Table 5.1, Policies I, II, III) stems from improvements associated with missioning more accurately in relation to local market quality as determined by local economic conditions, demographics, and other "supply" factors. To some extent, this is due to the fact that the mis-sioning approach utilized by USAREC during this period was reason-ably effective at accounting for these factors. The lion's share of the gains is due to greater responsiveness of effort to missions in stations that have been more successful recently.

- **The annual performance ratio we employed in the data analy-sis has desirable attributes, but alternative indicators should be considered.**

The data analysis measured recent performance by a station's total production of high-quality contracts divided by the total high-qual-ity mission during the 12-month period ending 3 months before the beginning of the current month. This measure has the advantages of (a) being implementable in real time (i.e., the required production data would be available almost three months before the missions depending on them would go into effect), and (b) tending to mitigate incentives to limit production in the interest of avoiding mission increases because of the lag and the averaging of 12 months of performance. Perhaps more importantly, we experimented with other definitions of "recent past performance," and none more effectively explained variations in contracts or led to qualitatively different predictions or interpretations.[5] Thus, we do not believe that any alternative measure would substan-tially improve the resulting reallocation from a short-term efficiency perspective. We are aware, however, that the design of a missioning

---

[5] For example, we used both longer and shorter windows (3- and 18-month periods) for performance. We also examined production regardless of mission. We used predicted proba-bilities of success for both regular Army and USAR missions in the current period (using the logistic regressions in Chapter Three to predict success). Finally, we examined the number of monthly successes in making regular Army mission box over the past year. None of these changes improved the fit of the model used in Chapter Four.

process and the manner in which it is communicated to the field raise leadership and morale issues that we haven't addressed.

- **The Army has used past performance in missioning, but these efforts could have been more effective.**

Previous versions of the Army missioning algorithm, at least at the battalion level, were based on past performance.[6] We demonstrated that during 2001 to 2003, missions were, in fact, adjusted in response to past performance (Table 5.2). However, this adjustment, simulated as Policy IX, produces a gain in high-quality contracts of only 0.6 percent, compared with a potential 2.7 percent improvement from Policy III (Table 5.1), about 80 percent of which comes from exploiting differences in effort functions associated with differences in recent past performance.

- **The addition of DEP losses to missions to create performance goals did not undermine productivity during 2001 to 2003, but this policy should be reviewed.**

DEP losses imbedded in the stations' goals were important in determining levels of contract production. In particular, variations in DEP losses account for about 20 percent of the variation in high-quality contracts, and they were roughly two-thirds as important as variation in missions in that regard (Table 4.2). Thus, we simulated a policy (Policy IV, Table 5.1) under which DEP losses are not added to missions when and where they occurred, but, instead, *expected* DEP losses were built into the missions for all stations.

---

[6] Although our preferred allocation scheme assigns missions at the station level, any battalion-level allocations are filtered down to the units below them. In the past, brigades' and battalions' shares of command-level missions were based in part on their average production levels over the past 36 months. (See the Addendum at the end of Chapter Four about how USAREC has determined missions in recent years.) However, these measures were included in USAREC missioning models primarily as proxies for economic and other market-quality factors. Because our model (Chapter Four) includes measures of a large number of such factors, little information of practical significance is gained from the inclusion of this 36-month production rate. More specifically, this was indicated by an analysis of the unexplained portions of contracts (i.e., the "regression residuals") from Model II in Chapter Four.

The results indicated that, under the mission allocation scheme used at the time, contracts were slightly higher because DEP losses were treated as increases in goals. This is due to a positive correlation between past performance and DEP losses. More specifically, more past success by a station tends to increase the size of its current delayed entry pool, larger DEPs tend to lead to more DEP losses and, as a result, higher performance goals for stations that respond more to higher mission. So, in the absence of effective adjustments for past performance, the inclusion of DEP losses in goals improved production. The key point, however, is that if missions are allocated efficiently on the basis of past performance, then the inclusion of DEP losses in goals may no longer be effective in increasing high-quality enlistments.[7]

- **A large portion of the short-term variation in enlistments is due to randomness.**

The model of station performance explains just over 40 percent of the variation in monthly enlistment outcomes (Figure 5.1). However, the fit is much better when the data are aggregated over months, reaching an R-squared of 82 percent for data aggregated over 12 months (Figure 5.1). Allowing for station-specific effects that are constant over time within the sample period brings the R-squared up to 92 percent. This suggests that missions might be best specified for periods longer than one month (e.g., a quarter), because performance assessments based on longer time intervals would be less sensitive to random events.

Promotion Prospects and Incentives for Recruiting

Recruiters appear to be highly motivated to be productive by pride in accomplishment, a drive to succeed, awards such as badges and stars, and other forms of recognition. Interviewees indicate, however, that

---

[7]   As we argue in Chapter Five, if one is concerned with encouraging activities to limit DEP losses, there are more direct ways to do so without affecting the marginal incentives to produce additional contracts in the current period.

being assigned to recruiting is believed to be a "career killer" in terms of prospects for promotion. This belief is likely to reduce soldiers' propensities to volunteer for recruiting and may undermine the morale and productivity of volunteer and DA-selected recruiters alike. In Chapter Six we analyzed several relationships between recruiting and soldiers' careers.

- **On average, becoming a recruiter increases promotion and retention rates.**

Controlling for entry year, earlier career success, occupation, and an extensive set of personal attributes, we found that individuals who become recruiters are more likely to become E-6s and E-7s (Tables 6.3, 6.4). They are also more likely to stay in the Army, even after leaving recruiting (Table 6.14).

- **Recruiters who perform well relative to their peers are promoted faster.**

We used a variety of performance measures, including the length of recruiting service, the performance of the recruiter's station relative to mission, and production rates, to consider how performance in recruiting affects a soldier's promotion prospects. For the latter two types of measures, we considered both levels of performance and performance relative to prevailing averages for all stations during the same time periods. Relative station performance, but not absolute performance, is highly predictive of promotion, length of service as a recruiter, and retention (Tables 6.11, 6.13). The implied effects are large and statistically significant. Although it is impossible for us to judge whether the magnitudes of the promotion-prospect rewards are about the right size, it is clear that there is a significant incentive in the form of improved promotion prospects for recruiters who are productive.

Identifying and Dealing with Unproductive New Recruiters

About 22 percent of soldiers who are assigned to recruiting duty remain in recruiting for less than one year (Table 6.2). Many of them are screened out of recruiting because of lack of productivity. Our analysis can be helpful in developing policies to deal with recruiters who continually fail to meet their production targets.

- **Screening recruiters on the basis of short-term performance is subject to considerable error.**

The high level of randomness in making mission box makes it quite difficult to identify good and bad recruiters on the basis of whether they consistently make or fail to make mission even over six months or more. Comparisons of predicted and actual probabilities of success (Table 3.11) indicate that many of the recruiters who have failed to make their missions over several consecutive months failed because of chance events, and that their recent low productivity is not predictive of low future productivity. Even among recruiters who have failed for 6 consecutive months, our analysis indicates that at least half are likely to be average or better recruiters who have low production levels because of some combination of unusually high missions, poor markets, or bad luck.

- **A sound management policy is to replace recruiters who are consistently unproductive during their first several months, but not to punish them. The Army appears to be doing this.**

Although large proportions of recruiters who consistently underproduce might not deserve negative personnel actions, it might make sense to replace them. First, some of the underperformers are unproductive for reasons that predict future lack of productivity. Second, even underperformers who are really average or better recruiters might be unproductive in the future because of the effects of low past productivity on morale and future effort levels. However, this does not imply that it is fair to punish unproductive recruiters who appear to be putting forth high levels of effort. Our evidence indicates that these individuals did not have significantly lower (or higher) promotion rates (Table 6.9, 6.10) than other recruiters. Thus, it does appear that the Army is applying sound management practices by returning them to their original jobs and not slowing their career progressions in those jobs. To confirm this result, it would be necessary to track the career paths of such individuals for a longer period of time than was possible in this study.

Conclusion

The analyses reported here exploit unusually detailed (i.e., station-level) data and new econometric models to analyze many issues with practical implications for the Army's recruiter-management policies. In particular, using data through June 2003, we have developed new empirical information that can be helpful in selecting recruiters, deciding where to assign them, and setting missions to increase aggregate high-quality enlistments and to promote equity across stations. Although the productivity gains may appear small in isolation, taken together the implementation of a broad range of modest policy changes could lead to quite dramatic improvements in overall efficiency of Army recruiting. Of course, the recruiting environment is ever changing because of developments in the youth labor market and the national security environment. Thus, we believe that the issues studied here should be periodically reexamined with the most recent data available.

In addition, we believe that station-level data and the econometric specifications developed here provide a promising foundation for studying a variety of questions that we have not addressed in this study. These include (a) the effects of military advertising and other marketing efforts on recruiting production, (b) the market expansion effects of a variety of enlistment benefits, and (c) the extent to which recruiting efforts by other services affect the production of Army recruiters.

Supplemental Statistical Analyses

This appendix documents a variety of supplemental analyses that were conducted in support of our research. Table A.1 shows results from a linear regression model used to impute the 1999 Army market share for about 10 percent of stations where data were missing. Table A.2 provides the results of a logistic regression predicting the probability of a station achieving zero, one, two, or three (or more) high-quality contracts. In Table A.3 we examine the share of females as a percentage of high-quality contracts. Table A.4 examines station-level productivity overall, while Tables A.5 through A.7 estimate several logistic models reported in the text for individual years. A variety of additional specification tests are provided in Tables A.8 through A.10. Table A.8 examines time trends in station productivity, and Table A.9 describes station productivity by recruiter cohort. Finally, Table A.10 reports regressions exploring the link between station performance and individual career outcomes.

Table A.1
Linear Regression Model Used to Impute 1999 Army Market Share When Actual Share Is Missing

	Variable	Coefficient	Standard Error
Intercept		49.5041	2.5814
S_m	High-quality senior mission per recruiter	0.2725	0.1332
G_m	High-quality graduate mission per recruiter	0.4538	0.0867
S_d	Senior DEP attrition per recruiter	0.5089	0.1614
G_d	Graduate DEP attrition per recruiter	0.2678	0.1561
x_1	2-recruiter station	0.7181	0.1480
x_2	3-recruiter station	1.3148	0.1855
x_3	4-recruiter station	1.7350	0.2276
x_4	5-recruiter station	2.1241	0.3165
x_5	6+ recruiter station	2.8722	0.5942
x_6	Reserve recruiters	0.6367	0.1597
x_8	Reserve mission, prior service	−0.0711	0.1050
x_9	Reserve mission, high school	0.5409	0.5419
x_{10}	DEP loss, "other" reserves	0.7641	0.2322
x_{11}	DEP loss, prior service reserves	−1.4484	1.5935
x_{12}	DEP loss, high school reserves	−0.2379	0.1778
x_{13}	Mission, "other" regular army	0.6882	0.0823
x_{14}	February	0.1000	0.2029
x_{15}	March	−0.0330	0.2299
x_{16}	April	0.0025	0.2387
x_{17}	May	0.2847	0.2280
x_{18}	June	0.3207	0.2164
x_{19}	July	−0.2320	0.2301
x_{20}	August	0.0310	0.2342
x_{21}	September	−0.4029	0.2257
x_{22}	October	−0.1284	0.2197
x_{23}	November	0.1535	0.2154
x_{24}	December	0.1299	0.2211
x_{25}	Mountain	1.6153	0.2770
x_{26}	North Central	−3.1912	0.1660
x_{27}	South	−1.9699	0.1995

Table A.1—continued

Variable		Coefficient	Standard Error
x_{28}	Pacific	−0.7974	0.2422
x_{29}	Hot	−0.0029	0.0007
x_{30}	Rain	0.0074	0.0005
x_{31}	Humidity	−0.0168	0.0052
x_{32}	Commanders, on production	−0.5272	0.1808
x_{33}	Recruiters on duty	1.8930	0.3179
x_{34}	Absent recruiters	0.9222	0.1339
x_{35}	Commanders, not on production	−0.8034	0.3245
x_{36}	QMA per recruiter	−1.4525	0.1037
x_{37}	Unemployment change	0.1210	0.4715

Table A.2
**Logistic Regression of Four Ordered High-Quality
Contract Outcomes**

Values of Dependent Variable	HQ Contracts	Percent
	0	0.5021
	1	0.3517
	2	0.1149
	3 or more	0.0313

Variable	Coefficient	Standard Error
Intercept 1	2.3164	0.2618
Intercept 2	4.1172	0.2620
Intercept 3	5.8059	0.2624
Mission	−0.2338	0.0075
Station variables:		
Two recruiters	0.1012	0.0405
Three recruiters	0.1317	0.0395
Four recruiters	0.2151	0.0396
Five recruiters	0.2206	0.0402
Six or more recruiters	0.2566	0.0409
Time variables:		
October	0.0765	0.0266
November	−0.1260	0.0262
December	0.2228	0.0270
January	0.1819	0.0270
February	−0.2341	0.0259
March	−0.0621	0.0261
April	−0.2431	0.0259
May	−0.0926	0.0266
June	−0.0071	0.0267
July	−0.0092	0.0266
August	−0.0414	0.0266
Fiscal year 1999	0.1128	0.0128
Fiscal year 2000	−0.0588	0.0177
Regional variables:		
Mountain	−0.0232	0.0281
North Central	0.0279	0.0186
South	0.0371	0.0168
Pacific	0.0022	0.0234
Market variables:		
QMA	−0.00009	0.00002
Unemployment	−0.0385	0.0157
Wage	0.3375	0.0485
College Enrollment	0.0068	0.0015

Table A.3
Linear Regression Results for Female High-Quality Recruits as a Percentage of High-Quality Contracts

Variable	Coefficient	Standard Error
Intercept	0.0191	0.0743
Mission	−0.0096	0.0021
2-recruiter station	0.0004	0.0111
3-recruiter station	0.0011	0.0108
4-recruiter station	−0.0066	0.0109
5-recruiter station	−0.0064	0.0111
6-plus recruiter station	0.0053	0.0112
October	−0.0039	0.0076
November	−0.0055	0.0074
December	−0.0092	0.0078
January	0.0082	0.0078
February	−0.0196	0.0073
March	−0.0067	0.0074
April	−0.0085	0.0073
May	−0.0048	0.0076
June	0.0020	0.0076
July	0.0112	0.0076
August	0.0029	0.0075
Fiscal year 1999	−0.0025	0.0037
Fiscal year 2000	−0.0127	0.0050
Mountain	−0.0021	0.0079
North Central	−0.0019	0.0053
South	−0.0001	0.0048
Pacific	−0.0070	0.0066
QMA per recruiter	0.0000	0.0000
log(unemployment)	0.0191	0.0044
log(civilian/military wage)	−0.0263	0.0138
Vet pop < 33	0.2381	0.0523
Vet pop 33–42	0.1016	0.0375
Vet pop 43–55	−0.0978	0.0240
Vet pop 56–65	0.0966	0.0392

Table A.3—continued

Variable	Coefficient	Standard Error
Vet pop 65–72	−0.1657	0.0472
Vet pop 73+	0.0824	0.0198
Competition	0.0008	0.0002
College percentage	−0.0001	0.0004
Black population	0.0508	0.0181
Hispanic population	−0.0176	0.0104
Cat I-II	−0.0100	0.0065
Cat IIIA	−0.0054	0.0065
Cat IIIB	−0.0128	0.0063
Black recruiter	0.0058	0.0057
Hispanic recruiter	0.0213	0.0125
Other race	−0.0009	0.0068
High school	0.0221	0.0230
College	0.0198	0.0326
Single	−0.0056	0.0058
Dependents	−0.0055	0.0041
Female	0.0693	0.0066
Young	−0.0033	0.0038
Older	−0.0013	0.0043
Technical	0.0098	0.0051
Intel	−0.0004	0.0147
Combat	0.0036	0.0049
Other	0.0099	0.0055
Career recruiter	0.0125	0.0068
Home state	0.0031	0.0035
Interactions:		
Black*Black population	0.1321	0.0237
Hispanic*Hispanic population	−0.0513	0.0270
College*College population	−0.00003	0.00055

Mean value = .2306.

Table A.4
Linear Regression Results: Station-Level Production of High-Quality Contracts

Variable	Coefficient	Standard Error
Intercept	−2.5381	0.2394
Station mission	0.2479	0.0019
2-recruiter station	0.3106	0.0405
3-recruiter station	0.6368	0.0397
4-recruiter station	0.8666	0.0401
5-recruiter station	1.1547	0.0411
6-plus recruiter station	1.5783	0.0428
October	−0.0214	0.0260
November	0.2795	0.0259
December	−0.2994	0.0262
January	−0.3174	0.0262
February	0.2250	0.0257
March	−0.2545	0.0259
April	0.1049	0.0259
May	0.1479	0.0261
June	0.0817	0.0263
July	0.1263	0.0262
August	0.2746	0.0262
Fiscal year 1999	−0.3092	0.0125
Fiscal year 2000	0.2047	0.0173
Mountain	0.0017	0.0277
North Central	−0.0235	0.0182
South	−0.0525	0.0163
Pacific	−0.0061	0.0230
QMA per recruiter	0.0002	0.0000
log(unemployment)	0.1237	0.0154
log(civilian/military wage)	−0.3810	0.0476
College population	−0.0125	0.0010

Table A.4—continued

Variable	Coefficient	Standard Error
Vet pop < 33	−0.9769	0.1814
Vet pop 33–42	1.0914	0.1303
Vet pop 43–55	−0.0256	0.0832
Vet pop 56–64	−0.0825	0.1348
Vet pop 65–72	−0.3622	0.1632
Vet pop 73+	−0.0261	0.0692
Competition	0.0402	0.0007
Black population	−0.4807	0.0453
Hispanic population	0.1815	0.0334

Tables A.5 and A.6 present a series of logistic regressions examining the probability of promotion to E-6 and E-7 for each year from 1987 through 1996. Coefficients should be interpreted as the change in the probability of *not* being promoted to E-6 and E-7. Table A.7 analyzes annual recruiter selection probabilities for the same time period. In Table A.8 we analyze time trends in average station performance. Table A.9 shows models examining the links between station productivity and the tenure of recruiters. Finally, Table A.10 presents regressions that quantify the correlation between relative station performance and career tenure of recruiters.

Table A.5
Probability of Not Being Promoted to E-6: Annual Logistic Probability Model Estimate

Cohort	1987		1988		1989		1990		1991	
Frequency	E-6 = 0	E-6 = 1	E-6 = 0	E-6 = 1	E-6 = 0	E-6 = 1	E-6 = 0	E-6 = 1	E-6 = 0	E-6 = 1
Observations	521	6,885	738	6,233	1,311	6,310	1,771	6,205	1,775	4,356
	Coeff.	Std. Error	Coeff.	Std. Error	Coeff.	Std. Error	Coeff.	Std. Error	Coeff.	Std. Error
intercept	-8.9704	0.9100	-9.5037	0.8288	-9.8951	0.6222	-10.0469	0.6334	-9.9576	0.7653
grade4	0.9317	0.0811	1.1180	0.0764	1.1582	0.0698	1.1990	0.0636	1.1386	0.0684
grade5	1.2347	0.1043	1.4745	0.0903	1.6725	0.0734	1.9103	0.0718	1.8737	0.0767
depend	-0.7648	0.1005	-0.7740	0.0895	-0.7496	0.0728	-0.5301	0.0657	-0.5321	0.0698
marry	-0.0636	0.1060	-0.1487	0.1094	-0.1260	0.0940	-0.4224	0.0827	-0.3290	0.0924
afqt	-0.1313	0.1585	-0.3325	0.1378	-0.2800	0.1105	-0.3496	0.1082	-0.3030	0.1157
grad	-0.1378	0.2959	0.0989	0.3562	-0.1062	0.1566	-0.3186	0.2277	0.2730	0.4152
college	-0.1718	0.1826	0.1829	0.1672	-0.3820	0.1672	-0.1961	0.1274	-0.4294	0.1474
white	0.4078	0.1099	0.3012	0.0981	0.3308	0.0782	0.1849	0.0694	0.1711	0.0716
male	0.2336	0.1672	0.1977	0.1290	0.1350	0.1033	-0.0274	0.0957	0.0908	0.1035
infantry	-0.9415	0.1890	-0.8921	0.1739	-1.0261	0.1365	-1.1612	0.1260	-1.2826	0.1301
armor	-1.4419	0.4320	-1.0355	0.2651	-0.6488	0.1901	-0.6756	0.1726	-0.8746	0.1770
artillery	-0.5130	0.1970	-0.4507	0.1797	-0.6112	0.1474	-0.6503	0.1251	-0.8282	0.1389
signal	-0.8168	0.2409	-0.8870	0.2164	-0.7173	0.1470	-0.4552	0.1415	-0.5797	0.1537
admin	-0.0491	0.2209	-0.0199	0.2031	0.0379	0.1427	0.1818	0.1215	-0.2678	0.1316
technical	0.0792	0.2106	0.4279	0.1814	0.1109	0.1680	0.4904	0.1455	0.0252	0.1541
munitions	-0.2491	0.5515	-1.1247	0.6322	-1.1632	0.4450	-1.5579	0.3663	-0.7843	0.2694
supply	0.1903	0.1799	0.3249	0.1659	0.4666	0.1318	0.5901	0.1261	0.5205	0.1354
medical	0.2418	0.1794	0.4788	0.1602	0.3069	0.1389	-0.0294	0.1271	-0.0579	0.1147
police	-0.5058	0.3017	-0.5255	0.2662	-0.6412	0.2398	-0.4479	0.1929	-0.8365	0.2070
food	-0.1243	0.2464	-0.2349	0.2789	-0.0924	0.2219	-0.0355	0.1687	-0.1329	0.2021
intel	-2.4798	1.0134	-0.6132	0.3042	-1.0495	0.2874	-0.9491	0.3287	-0.8282	0.3038
transport	0.3150	0.2451	0.6328	0.1990	0.7604	0.1538	0.3248	0.1594	0.1797	0.1870
other	-0.7090	0.2519	-0.5384	0.2043	-0.5866	0.1603	-0.3308	0.1498	-0.8639	0.2014
recruiter	-0.9468	0.1779	-1.2179	0.1739	-0.9196	0.1341	-0.7575	0.1177	-0.8234	0.1365

Table A.5—continued

Cohort	1992		1993		1994		1995		1996	
Frequency	E-6 = 0	E-6 = 1	E-6 = 0	E-6 = 1	E-6 = 0	E-6 = 1	E-6 = 0	E-6 = 1	E-6 = 0	E-6 = 1
Observations	3,070	4,976	3,327	4,379	3,897	3,632	4,912	3,157	7,503	2,527
	Coeff.	Std. Error	Coeff.	Std. Error	Coeff.	Std. Error	Coeff.	Std. Error	Coeff.	Std. Error
intercept	-8.6996	0.6839	-7.7166	0.5710	-7.4591	0.5916	-6.1296	0.7144	-6.3919	0.5876
grade4	1.1447	0.0618	1.1110	0.0610	1.2049	0.0672	0.9395	0.0723	1.1549	0.0816
grade5	1.9522	0.0618	1.7171	0.0567	1.7763	0.0574	1.8797	0.0597	2.0449	0.0628
depend	-0.3709	0.0575	-0.4272	0.0564	-0.3423	0.0563	-0.3172	0.0551	-0.3322	0.0548
marry	-0.2202	0.0696	-0.3842	0.0680	-0.3990	0.0724	-0.4107	0.0701	-0.2847	0.0680
afqt	-0.5718	0.0940	-0.3836	0.0925	-0.4689	0.0942	-0.5640	0.0909	-0.5798	0.0867
grad	0.1818	0.4562	-0.3179	0.2751	-0.2053	0.2983	0.3307	0.5228	0.5560	0.2740
college	-0.3228	0.1036	-0.5155	0.1025	-0.5738	0.0972	-0.4573	0.0972	-0.6426	0.0988
white	0.0176	0.0589	0.0723	0.0592	0.1694	0.0608	0.1590	0.0588	0.0769	0.0580
male	0.0866	0.0781	0.2030	0.0808	0.1535	0.0825	0.0812	0.0850	-0.00168	0.0851
infantry	-1.1449	0.1121	-0.8660	0.0970	-1.0501	0.0962	-1.3201	0.0970	-1.2681	0.0961
armor	-0.7139	0.1734	-0.3096	0.1496	-0.6564	0.1266	-0.7126	0.1119	-0.6257	0.1290
artillery	-0.7027	0.1098	-0.7716	0.1081	-0.5428	0.1047	-1.0219	0.0995	-0.9569	0.1015
signal	-0.9298	0.1479	-0.7029	0.1699	-0.7053	0.1492	-0.7741	0.1343	-0.6712	0.1223
admin	-0.2124	0.1015	0.0450	0.1025	0.1680	0.1137	-0.2826	0.1489	0.2515	0.1408
technical	-0.0443	0.1197	0.1017	0.1200	-0.1255	0.1262	-0.0249	0.1489	-0.2745	0.1387
munitions	-1.0024	0.3402	-0.7119	0.3536	-0.8806	0.3072	-0.9342	0.3277	-1.1750	0.2669
supply	0.5132	0.1026	0.6416	0.1109	0.7508	0.1161	0.4101	0.1319	0.3510	0.1277
medical	0.0968	0.0948	0.2533	0.1048	0.3881	0.1231	-0.1600	0.1261	-0.1383	0.1431
police	-0.6052	0.1747	-0.3561	0.1512	-0.4920	0.1488	-0.4622	0.1451	-0.3475	0.1305
food	-0.0856	0.1591	0.2596	0.2059	0.2919	0.1836	0.1095	0.2651	7.2283	196.40
intel	-0.8941	0.2972	-0.7038	0.1865	-0.7982	0.1706	-1.2146	0.1595	-1.2827	0.1464
transport	0.3688	0.1443	0.3438	0.1485	0.2835	0.1717	0.6187	0.1646	0.6368	0.2236
other	-0.7041	0.1516	-0.4023	0.1234	-0.4854	0.1282	-0.7029	0.1221	-0.6933	0.1176
recruiter	-0.7978	0.1172	-0.6449	0.1087	-0.6618	0.1185	-0.3196	0.1116	-0.2762	0.1103

Table A.6
Probability of Not Being Promoted to E-7: Annual Logistic Probability Model Estimates

Cohort	1987		1988		1989		1990		1991		1992		1993	
Frequency	E-7 = 0	E-7 = 1	E-7 = 0	E-7 = 1	E-7 = 0	E-7 = 1	E-7 = 0	E-7 = 1	E-7 = 0	E-7 = 1	E-7 = 0	E-7 = 1	E-7 = 0	E-7 = 1
Obs.	3,770	3,636	4,133	2,838	5,541	2,080	6,394	1,582	5,336	772	7,551	495	7,466	240
	Coeff.	Std. Error	Coeff.	Std. Error	Coeff.	Std. Error	Coeff.	Std. Error	Coeff.	Std. Error	Coeff.	Std. Error	Coeff.	Std. Error
intercept	-5.6563	0.4896	-6.5621	0.5489	-6.5704	0.5274	-6.4168	0.6850	-6.3673	1.0905	-6.8863	1.2004	-2.3555	1.7843
grade4	0.8339	0.0474	1.0559	0.0541	1.2205	0.0633	1.2330	0.0674	1.3404	0.0963	1.3887	0.1186	1.2978	0.1741
grade5	1.3175	0.0543	1.6195	0.0626	1.8777	0.0616	2.0445	0.0670	2.1803	0.0910	2.4166	0.1156	2.2661	0.1553
depend	0.00683	0.0602	-0.00286	0.0638	0.00509	0.0686	0.0889	0.0736	-0.2097	0.1014	-0.2546	0.1174	-0.3274	0.1604
marry	-0.1194	0.0560	-0.1848	0.0680	-0.2797	0.0778	-0.1710	0.0798	-0.1514	0.1197	-0.0876	0.1329	0.0608	0.1773
afqt	-0.3743	0.0841	-0.4854	0.0880	-0.6328	0.0942	-0.5244	0.1137	-0.5555	0.1630	-0.8822	0.1942	-1.1042	0.2679
grad	-0.0913	0.1727	-0.0873	0.2435	-0.2613	0.1497	-0.7278	0.3327	-0.6014	0.6475	1.7193	0.5894	-0.3351	1.0297
college	-0.1474	0.0852	0.1223	0.0984	-0.1423	0.1073	-0.2816	0.1043	-0.3569	0.1471	-0.7207	0.1430	-0.6866	0.1798
white	0.0579	0.0591	-0.0299	0.0632	0.0297	0.0682	-0.1654	0.0737	-0.0998	0.1022	-0.3200	0.1245	-0.5234	0.1760
male	0.0675	0.0892	0.1605	0.0896	-0.0194	0.0973	-0.1054	0.1165	0.0141	0.1631	-0.1151	0.1893	0.3167	0.2405
infantry	-0.3240	0.0930	-0.2955	0.0988	-0.3720	0.1033	-0.5804	0.1155	-0.6044	0.1652	-1.0114	0.1897	-0.4828	0.2611
armor	-0.3271	0.1448	-0.5242	0.1300	-0.2600	0.1421	-0.1353	0.1531	-0.3588	0.2013	-0.0747	0.2950	0.0893	0.3833
artillery	0.0687	0.1012	-0.1840	0.1102	-0.3042	0.1196	-0.2315	0.1328	-0.3291	0.1929	-0.7019	0.2159	-0.9429	0.2702
signal	-0.2454	0.1169	-0.4490	0.1229	-0.4137	0.1252	-0.5962	0.1508	-0.4564	0.2210	-0.3486	0.2699	0.2583	0.5600
admin	-0.4404	0.1242	-0.4605	0.1370	-0.2494	0.1373	-0.5928	0.1450	-0.4218	0.2058	-0.5153	0.2331	-0.6859	0.3039
technical	0.1311	0.1311	0.1074	0.1390	0.1289	0.1604	0.2377	0.1802	0.5115	0.2701	0.2013	0.2853	-0.1640	0.3614
munitions	-0.3152	0.2888	-0.5359	0.3210	-0.9207	0.3609	-0.7501	0.2946	0.3919	0.5417	-0.6984	0.5860	0.2806	1.0558
supply	0.1770	0.1127	-0.1561	0.1275	0.00112	0.1431	0.2318	0.1865	0.1930	0.2586	-0.3863	0.2513	-0.0566	0.4088
medical	0.1126	0.1097	0.3178	0.1280	0.3587	0.1393	0.1372	0.1567	0.1230	0.1945	0.0142	0.2252	0.4842	0.3797
police	0.3142	0.1533	0.2254	0.1602	0.1970	0.2064	-0.2326	0.2252	-0.2037	0.2993	0.0610	0.4023	-0.4909	0.3994
food	-0.0348	0.1450	-0.4268	0.1925	-0.2900	0.2075	-0.3552	0.2065	-0.7087	0.2930	0.4583	0.4694	0.1559	0.7592
intel	-0.1026	0.1915	-0.1350	0.1649	-0.1904	0.1650	-0.1511	0.2173	-0.3673	0.2503	-0.1537	0.3520	-0.5783	0.3369
transport	0.5656	0.1699	0.3869	0.1614	0.6813	0.1706	0.5528	0.2286	0.1349	0.3123	0.1654	0.3993	0.5382	0.6283
other	0.0416	0.1234	-0.2562	0.1256	-0.2994	0.1259	-0.0217	0.1606	-0.4470	0.2292	-0.2508	0.2840	-0.3210	0.3379
recruiter	-0.1799	0.0678	-0.3212	0.0723	-0.1052	0.0801	-0.2256	0.0856	-0.2925	0.1223	-0.2672	0.1516	-0.2846	0.1998

Table A.7
Probability of Not Being Selected for Recruiting: Annual Logistic Probability Model Estimates

Cohort	1987		1988		1989		1990		1991	
Frequency	REC = 0	REC = 1	REC = 0	REC = 1	REC = 0	REC = 1	REC = 0	REC = 1	REC = 0	REC = 1
Observations	6,173	1,233	5,870	1,101	6,562	1,059	6,912	1,064	5,472	636
	Coeff.	Std. Error	Coeff.	Std. Error	Coeff.	Std. Error	Coeff.	Std. Error	Coeff.	Std. Error
intercept	2.0668	0.6123	2.6994	0.6846	2.8257	0.6044	2.4709	0.7642	1.1976	0.9268
grade4	0.1296	0.0571	0.2778	0.0628	0.3098	0.0681	0.4792	0.0663	0.3277	0.0850
grade5	0.1890	0.0614	0.1081	0.0674	0.3675	0.0622	0.5199	0.0620	0.5416	0.0799
depend	0.2682	0.0728	0.0703	0.0743	0.1605	0.0773	0.2292	0.0745	0.0891	0.0946
marry	0.0363	0.0707	0.0791	0.0852	-0.0750	0.0899	-0.00667	0.0854	-0.1316	0.1149
afqt	-0.2316	0.1048	-0.3893	0.1076	-0.6039	0.1089	-0.5326	0.1180	-0.4465	0.1550
grad	-0.4040	0.2348	-0.5345	0.3565	-0.2998	0.1788	-1.3534	0.4619	0.4458	0.4309
college	0.3507	0.1159	0.2103	0.1270	-0.0230	0.1282	0.0967	0.1200	-0.0953	0.1588
white	-0.0677	0.0744	-0.1157	0.0778	0.0363	0.0785	-0.1139	0.0775	-0.1878	0.0991
male	-0.4763	0.1350	-0.3251	0.1230	-0.4434	0.1290	-0.4064	0.1362	-0.3369	0.1791
infantry	0.0669	0.1156	-0.2503	0.1211	-0.6002	0.1229	-0.5061	0.1230	-0.5021	0.1593
armor	-0.6336	0.1569	-0.3288	0.1576	-0.8943	0.1548	-0.5396	0.1576	-0.7608	0.1887
artillery	-0.4927	0.1171	-0.4767	0.1319	-0.8979	0.1331	-0.5846	0.1338	-0.5328	0.1781
signal	-0.3015	0.1393	-0.4221	0.1466	-0.4691	0.1492	-0.3284	0.1634	-0.3121	0.2151
admin	0.2112	0.1709	0.0783	0.1865	-0.2503	0.1703	-0.2639	0.1594	-0.00118	0.2157
technical	0.2623	0.1757	0.2422	0.1900	-0.3069	0.1913	-0.0981	0.1894	-0.2022	0.2311
munitions	1.1139	0.5251	0.1438	0.4176	0.1032	0.5318	-0.7866	0.2814	0.0933	0.4418
supply	0.0657	0.1444	-0.0216	0.1664	-0.1959	0.1752	0.1122	0.1937	0.1288	0.2454
medical	0.3277	0.1495	0.0883	0.1615	0.0752	0.1770	0.2682	0.1800	0.0155	0.1868
police	-0.0506	0.1858	-0.3803	0.1814	-0.2990	0.2295	-0.5634	0.2078	-0.5642	0.2513
food	0.2534	0.1991	-0.1154	0.2554	-0.2198	0.2756	-0.1402	0.2351	-0.6379	0.2786
intel	1.6520	0.3982	0.4953	0.2277	0.3078	0.2387	0.4734	0.2932	0.4376	0.3344
transport	-0.1651	0.2001	-0.4572	0.1838	-0.5721	0.1772	-0.6379	0.1908	-0.4467	0.2662
other	0.4857	0.1710	0.1600	0.1647	-0.2583	0.1580	-0.2278	0.1678	-0.1884	0.2420

Table A.7—continued

Cohort	1992		1993		1994		1995		1996	
Frequency	REC = 0	REC = 1	REC = 0	REC = 1	REC = 0	REC = 1	REC = 0	REC = 1	REC = 0	REC = 1
Observations	7,389	657	7,075	631	7,067	462	7,609	460	9,571	459
	Coeff.	Std. Error	Coeff.	Std. Error	Coeff.	Std. Error	Coeff.	Std. Error	Coeff.	Std. Error
intercept	2.7948	1.3000	3.1667	0.9708	3.6335	1.0692	4.0347	1.2134	4.6919	1.1475
grade4	0.3964	0.0915	0.4664	0.0971	0.4108	0.1157	0.5110	0.1272	0.5946	0.1455
grade5	0.6207	0.0815	0.6247	0.0806	0.5455	0.0927	0.7983	0.0984	0.7830	0.1039
depend	0.1105	0.0898	0.1676	0.0896	0.1035	0.1019	0.0352	0.1020	0.1610	0.0995
marry	0.0287	0.1091	0.0855	0.1106	-0.00983	0.1324	-0.0738	0.1327	0.0834	0.1349
afqt	-0.6322	0.1501	-0.8930	0.1527	-0.8496	0.1760	-1.1474	0.1762	-1.1655	0.1695
grad	-0.7332	1.0267	-0.3884	0.5210	-0.1188	0.5279	0.3288	0.7684	-0.2340	0.5981
college	-0.00383	0.1458	-0.0837	0.1410	-0.1825	0.1582	0.2630	0.1893	0.0752	0.1973
white	-0.1803	0.0964	0.0129	0.0977	-0.1591	0.1150	-0.1275	0.1135	-0.1013	0.1110
male	-0.4024	0.1613	-0.3812	0.1603	-0.3148	0.1902	-0.4698	0.2066	-0.6249	0.2077
infantry	-0.5169	0.1467	-0.4687	0.1458	-0.7640	0.1608	-1.0934	0.1958	-0.8520	0.1847
armor	-0.5665	0.2087	-0.3954	0.2106	-0.2711	0.2266	-0.9928	0.2162	-1.0206	0.2191
artillery	-0.6996	0.1552	-0.6209	0.1565	-0.4795	0.1902	-0.7206	0.2139	-0.8606	0.1925
signal	-0.1831	0.2104	-0.4240	0.2469	-0.1964	0.2662	-0.8180	0.2520	-0.6070	0.2268
admin	0.00432	0.1856	0.1331	0.1959	0.00596	0.2348	-0.7992	0.2735	-0.0603	0.2940
technical	-0.3421	0.1900	-0.2231	0.2002	0.2609	0.2800	-0.6709	0.3025	-0.2449	0.2900
munitions	-0.0213	0.5336	-0.5721	0.4554	0.3168	0.7342	-1.2009	0.5080	0.2359	0.7347
supply	0.2785	0.2078	0.00264	0.2049	0.3169	0.2559	0.0819	0.3320	0.0534	0.2759
medical	0.4023	0.1853	0.4015	0.2093	0.5781	0.2871	0.7218	0.3961	0.5879	0.3904
police	-0.2200	0.2648	-0.3005	0.2406	-0.2533	0.2767	-0.2902	0.3150	-0.1255	0.2742
food	-0.0842	0.2903	0.4384	0.4716	1.2872	0.7240	-0.3919	0.6166	5.8017	258.80
intel	0.4278	0.3875	0.4212	0.2927	0.3446	0.3100	-0.4665	0.3012	0.3284	0.3587
transport	-0.3753	0.2367	-0.4917	0.2392	-0.7321	0.2812	-1.0519	0.2766	-0.7471	0.3253
other	0.0155	0.2358	-0.1545	0.1995	0.1673	0.2639	-0.6103	0.2548	-0.8203	0.2127

Table A.8
Time Trends in Average Station Performance,
1997–2002

Variable	Coefficient	Standard Error
Intercept	0.7879	0.0067
1998	−0.3561	0.0158
1999	0.0078	0.0156
2000	0.0929	0.0147
2001	0.3335	0.0119
2002	0.3151	0.0229

R-squared = 0.2809.

NOTE: Dependent variable is the number of high-quality contracts divided by the mission, with a mean of 0.838.

Table A.9
Models of Station Productivity, by Recruiter Cohort

Year	Duration	Coefficient	Standard Error
1997	< 1 year (baseline)	0.6073	0.0121
	< 2 years	−0.0495	0.0162
	< 3 years	−0.0341	0.0167
	< 4 years	0.0430	0.0255
	> 4 years	0.0882	0.0210
1998	< 1 year	−0.0281	0.0241
	< 2 years	0.0024	0.0278
	< 3 years	0.0725	0.0166
	< 4 years	0.1470	0.0223
	> 4 years	0.1351	0.0464
1999	< 1 year	0.1663	0.0269
	< 2 years	0.1515	0.0317
	< 3 years	0.2004	0.0156
	< 4 years	0.2210	0.0311
2000	< 1 year	0.2595	0.0245
	< 2 years	0.3630	0.0199
	< 3 years	0.3213	0.0247
2001	< 1 year	0.4604	0.0202
	< 2 years	0.4423	0.0267
2002	< 1 year	0.4764	0.0252

Table A.10
Regression Coefficients of Relative Station Performance in Determining Career Outcomes

Dependent Variable	Coefficient	Standard Error
Prob (tenure < 1 yr)	0.2021	0.0839
Prob (tenure < 2 yr)	−0.6192	0.0645
Prob (tenure < 3 yr)	−2.3646	0.0779
Prob (leaving 2003)	1.0653	0.0979

Data Sources

This appendix provides additional detail concerning the data utilized in this report. Table B.1 provides a list of data sources. All information regarding individual recruiters, their contract production, missions, and term of service was provided directly by the United States Recruiting Command from the Army Recruiting Information Support System. For career paths and characteristics of enlistment personnel, we relied on the Enlisted Master File (EMF).

Table B.2 provides codes for career management fields (CMFs) and a brief description of occupational specialties. For the studies reported in this document, groups of occupations were combined to reduce the number of parameters estimated in the various models. The combinations were somewhat arbitrary, but were meant to represent occupations with common attributes, for example, maintenance- or combat-related. In addition, some groupings were dictated by the results of exploratory empirical work in cases where the relationship between CMF and the outcome of interest appeared to be similar.

Table B.1
Data Sources

Contracts	Army Recruiting Information Support System—Mission Production Awards (ARISS-MPA), United States Army Recruiting Command
Career paths, characteristics of enlisted personnel	Enlisted Master File (EMF)
Missions	ARISS-MPA
Recruiters	ARISS-MPA
Personnel/staffing	ARISS-MPA
Unemployment rate	Bureau of Labor Statistics (http://stats/bls.gov)
Average hourly earnings	Bureau of Labor Statistics
Military wages	Defense Finance and Accounting Service (DFAS) (www.dfas.mil/money/milpay)
College enrollments	Current Population Survey (www.bls.census.gov/cps/bdata/htm)
Qualified military available (QMA)	Recruit Market Information System (RMIS), Defense Manpower Data Center
Population characteristics, race, gender, age, education	Woods & Poole (www.woodsandpoole.com)
Market demographics, urban, rural populations, income, poverty levels	U.S. Bureau of the Census (www.factfinder.census.gov)
Veteran counts by state and age group	Special tabulations provided by Veterans Administration
Religious affiliation	*Religious Congregations & Membership in the United States,* Glenmary Research Center
Army market share	Defense Manpower Data Center (DMDC)

Table B.2
Career Management Fields

Career Management Field	Description
9	Training
11	Infantry
12	Combat Engineering
13	Field Artillery
14	Air Defense Artillery
18	Special Forces
19	Armor
23	Air Defense System Maintenance
25	Visual Information
27	Land Combat and Air Defense System Maintenance
29	Signal Maintenance
31	Signal Operations
33	Electronic Warfare/Intercept Systems Maintenance
35	Electronic Maintenance and Calibration
37	Psychological Operations
46	Public Affairs
51	General Engineering
54	Chemical
55	Ammunition
63	Mechanical Maintenance
67	Aircraft Maintenance
71	Administration
74	Record Information Operations
76	Supply and Services
77	Petroleum and Water
79	Recruitment and Reenlistment
81	Topographical Engineering
88	Transportation
91	Medical
92	Supply and Services
93	Aviation Operations
94	Food Services
95	Military Police
96	Military Intelligence
97	Bands
98	Signals Intelligence/Electronic Warfare Operations

References

Asch, Beth J., and Lynn A. Karoly, *The Role of the Job Counselor in the Military Enlistment Process*, Santa Monica, CA: RAND, MR-315-P&R, 1993.

Chowdhury, Jhinuk, "The Motivational Impact of Sales Quotas on Effort," *Journal of Marketing Research*, Vol. XXX, February 1993, pp. 28–41.

Darmon, Rene Y., "Selecting Appropriate Sales Quota Plan Structures and Quota-Setting Procedures," *Journal of Personal Selling & Sales Management*, Vol. XVII, No. 1, Winter 1997, pp. 1–16.

Dertouzos, James N., *Recruiter Incentives and Enlistment Supply*, Santa Monica, CA: RAND, R-3065-MIL, May 1985.

Dertouzos, James N., and Steven Garber, *Is Military Advertising Effective? An Estimation Methodology and Applications to Recruiting in the 1980s and 90s*, Santa Monica, CA: RAND, MR-1591-OSD, 2003.

Hosek, James R., and Michael Mattock, *Learning About Quality, How the Quality of Military Personnel Is Revealed Over Time*, Santa Monica, CA: RAND, MR-1593-OSD, 2003.

Oken, Carole, and Beth J. Asch, *Encouraging Recruiter Achievement, A Recent History of Military Recruiter Incentive Programs*, Santa Monica, CA: RAND, MR-845-OSD/A, 1997.

Polich, J. Michael, James N. Dertouzos, and S. James Press, *The Enlistment Bonus Experiment*, Santa Monica, CA: RAND, R-3353-FMP, April 1986.

Tubbs, Mark E., "Goal Setting: A Meta-Analytic Examination of the Empirical Evidence," *Journal of Applied Psychology*, Vol. 71, No. 3, 1986, pp. 474–483.